# Recognition or Disagreement

NEW DIRECTIONS IN CRITICAL THEORY

# NEW DIRECTIONS IN CRITICAL THEORY

Amy Allen, General Editor

New Directions in Critical Theory presents outstanding classic and contemporary texts in the tradition of critical social theory, broadly construed. The series aims to renew and advance the program of critical social theory, with a particular focus on theorizing contemporary struggles around gender, race, sexuality, class, and globalization and their complex interconnections.

*Narrating Evil: A Postmetaphysical Theory of Reflective Judgment*, María Pía Lara

*The Politics of Our Selves: Power, Autonomy, and Gender in Contemporary Critical Theory*, Amy Allen

*Democracy and the Political Unconscious*, Noëlle McAfee

*The Force of the Example: Explorations in the Paradigm of Judgment*, Alessandro Ferrara

*Horrorism: Naming Contemporary Violence*, Adriana Cavarero

*Scales of Justice: Reimagining Political Space in a Globalizing World*, Nancy Fraser

*Pathologies of Reason: On the Legacy of Critical Theory*, Axel Honneth

*States Without Nations: Citizenship for Mortals*, Jacqueline Stevens

*The Racial Discourses of Life Philosophy: Négritude, Vitalism, and Modernity*, Donna V. Jones

*Democracy in What State?*, Giorgio Agamben, Alain Badiou, Daniel Bensaïd, Wendy Brown, Jean-Luc Nancy, Jacques Rancière, Kristin Ross, Slavoj Žižek

*Politics of Culture and the Spirit of Critique: Dialogues*, edited by Gabriel Rockhill and Alfredo Gomez-Muller

For a complete list of the series see page 231

# Recognition or Disagreement

JACQUES RANCIÈRE

AXEL HONNETH

A CRITICAL ENCOUNTER ON THE POLITICS OF FREEDOM, EQUALITY, AND IDENTITY

EDITED BY
KATIA GENEL AND
JEAN-PHILIPPE DERANTY

COLUMBIA UNIVERSITY PRESS
NEW YORK

Columbia University Press
*Publishers Since 1893*
New York Chichester, West Sussex
cup.columbia.edu


Chapter 7, "Of the Poverty of Our Liberty: The Greatness and Limits of Hegel's Doctrine of Ethical Life," was originally published in the German as "Von der Armut unserer Freiheit: Größe und Grenzen der Hegelschen Sittlichkeitslehre" © Suhrkamp Verlag Berlin.

Library of Congress Cataloging-in-Publication Data
Names: Honneth, Axel, 1949– author. | Rancière, Jacques, author. | Genel, Katia, editor.
Title: Recognition or disagreement : a critical encounter on the politics of freedom, equality, and identity / Axel Honneth and Jacques Rancière ; edited by Katia Genel and Jean-Philippe Deranty.
Description: New York : Columbia University Press, 2016. | Series: New directions in critical theory | Includes bibliographical references and index.
Identifiers: LCCN 2015039970 | ISBN 9780231177160 (cloth : alk. paper) | ISBN 9780231541442 (e-book)
Subjects: LCSH: Critical theory. | Political science—Philiosophy. | Honneth, Axel, 1949– | Rancière, Jacques. | Recognition (Philosophy)
Classification: LCC B809.3 .H667 2016 | DDC 320.092/2—dc23
LC record available at http://lccn.loc.gov/2015039970

Columbia University Press books are printed on permanent and durable acid-free paper.
Printed in the United States of America

Cover and book design: Lisa Hamm
Cover image: © Hermione Carline, *Illumination Dark*. Private Collection/Bridgeman Images

# CONTENTS

## PART III THE METHOD OF CRITICAL THEORY: PROPOSITIONS

# Recognition or Disagreement

# PART I

# Setting the Stage

one

# JACQUES RANCIÈRE AND AXEL HONNETH

## Two Critical Approaches to the Political

KATIA GENEL

### A BRIEF ENCOUNTER

AXEL HONNETH, the famous German theorist of recognition who took over the legacy of the Frankfurt School and especially of Jürgen Habermas, and Jacques Rancière, the eminent French thinker of the disagreement (*mésentente*) who broke with the Althusserian tradition, are two central figures in the contemporary intellectual landscape. Their thinking is located in two different traditions, but both deal with the heritage of Marxism, which they both consider in a highly critical way. Both thinkers have interest in specific areas inside and outside of philosophy. Both share a common concern for the political. However, while Axel Honneth approaches the political through arguments from social philosophy, moral philosophy, and philosophy of law and extensively refers to the social sciences, Jacques Rancière, for his part, turns to aesthetics and literature. A confrontation between these two influential modes of practicing critical thinking seems highly overdue. It is important for the field of contemporary critical theory to establish whether the paradigms Honneth and Rancière put forward to criticize contemporary society, to account for its evolution and for the transformations that can make it more just, are competing, whether they are mutually exclusive, or whether they are somehow compatible. To date, however, apart from a few studies conducted almost a decade ago, such a confrontation has still not really taken place.[1]

To this effect, a meeting was organized in June 2009 in Frankfurt am Main, in the historical building of the Institute for Social Research. Axel Honneth and Jacques Rancière initiated a discussion—moderated by the German Philosopher Christoph Menke—around the key theses of their best-known books, *The Struggle for Recognition* and *Disagreement*.[2] Each thinker began by "reconstructing" the theoretical position of his interlocutor. This issued in a debate on the underlying principles of the "critical theory" that each represents, a clarification of their methodological approaches to society and politics, and, finally, a discussion of the possibility of overcoming injustice and of a political transformation of society. Indeed, their discussion centered on the very meaning of "critical theory." It is a specific task of this volume to help elucidate this meaning.

This book is the result of this short and intense encounter between the two thinkers. What is published here are the texts presented by Honneth and Rancière, the theoretical exchange that took place between them, and a supplementary text from each author intended to provide a deeper understanding of their thinking, their theoretical orientations, and their methods. Honneth's method has a strong Hegelian spirit. It is marked by a specific way of discussing political issues—and here, more specifically, the political concept of freedom—through an approach he refers to as "social philosophy," that is to say, a philosophical type of analysis that takes society as an object and relies on the results of the social sciences. Rancière's method is a radical political questioning based on the principle whereby the social order is contested by any act that presupposes the equality of anyone with anyone and that verifies it (a "method of equality"). I believe that the short yet substantive discussions between the two thinkers represent a model and an excellent starting point for comparative studies into the possible ways of exercising social criticism, and that such comparative work is particularly apt to develop fruitful perspective onto many significant theoretical issues. Each of these practices shows important deficits in the other approach. One focuses on the need to transform society by the advent of *social* orders of recognition, the other on the affirmation of *politics*, assuming the irreversible division of the social. Thinking this divergence enlightens the reference to a critical approach in a large sense. This introduction discusses the texts published in this volume, and frames the confrontation between the two authors in relation to the main coordinates of their thinking. Jean-Philippe Deranty's discussion, by contrast, takes a broader focus and seeks to situate the two models in the overall theoretical landscape, highlighting problems and potentials that each of the two models raises in relation to the general project of a philosophical critique of contemporary society. A substantive bibliography with a specific focus on the confrontation between the "German" and the "French" traditions is provided at the end of the volume to assist students and researchers in comparative studies in critical theory.



## TWO CRITICAL THEORISTS?

While Honneth refers to the concept of freedom and Rancière uses equality as his central concept, both authors share the same fundamental concerns: they both question contemporary societies by asking about the conditions of justice. They both develop tools that are intended to help us understand the social mechanism that prevents the realization of justice and develop a theory to overcome injustice. Indeed, if we consider the appellation "critical theory" in a very broad sense, both authors can be linked to this tradition. But what is a point of connection between them is also a problem or a set of problems.

Criticism is understood not only in the sense of Kant—that of establishing the conditions of possibility of knowledge—but also in the sense of Marx, namely, as the articulation between theory and practice. It refers at the same time to the act of dispelling illusions that are constitutive of particular social conditions through the constitution of an emancipatory knowledge and to the thinking of the conditions of a free praxis. The critical tradition is not a unified or univocal tradition. Even in the narrow sense of what was retrospectively called the "Frankfurt School," it is complex: the succession of generations of thinkers is marked by forms of heritage and rupture, appropriations or actualizations that distort and displace the original theory in productive ways. Critical theory was initially the Marxist-inspired method reformulated by Horkheimer in the 1930s, around which he gathered the members of the Institute of Social Research (the members of what is called the "first generation" of the Frankfurt School). In 1937, Horkheimer defined critical theory, in opposition to traditional theory, as a self-reflexive theory, conscious of the social conditions in which it unfolds, and as aiming at their emancipatory transformation.[3] The name "critical theory" was then used as a way to disguise an unavowable reference to Marxism—although it was a renewed Marxism read in light of Hegel, against a positivist reading that was current in the discourses of political parties at the time. The idea was to develop a theory that would not accept the socioeconomic reality, and that could question the socioeconomic processes by performing an overall judgment on society and the direction it should take. At the beginning of the 1940s, considering that the sciences, even dialectically integrated into a general theory of social development, could not guarantee criticism anymore, the critical theory of the Frankfurt School took the new shape of a radical dialectic of Enlightenment, and later the shape of a "negative dialectic," as it was developed by Adorno.[4] Performing what is commonly referred to as the "linguistic turn," Habermas argued that the criticism of rationality that had so far been developed by the first generation of the Frankfurt School was too one-sided to provide a basis for a renewed theory of society and developed a theory of communicative rationality.

In parallel, a broader form of critical thinking emerged in Europe and in the United States. Critical theory in this broad sense is not a unified theory either, but rather a collection of different styles of critical thinking. Gender Studies, Subaltern or Postcolonial Studies, Ecological thinking, Feminism, and Neo-Marxism can all be placed within this broad current of thought, with thinkers as different as Althusser, Foucault, Lyotard, Deleuze, Derrida, Badiou, Negri, Balibar, Laclau, Mouffe, and Butler as their main representatives.[5] A section of this critical literature should be analyzed in relation to Marxism, and can be conceived at least as a criticism, if not as a sort of continuation of it. Many of these critical thinkers don't mention the Frankfurt School. Some of these critical thinkers have occasionally defined their position in reference to the Frankfurt theory: we can mention *The Postmodern Condition* of Lyotard and a few incidental remarks made by Foucault on his affinity with the Frankfurt School as he expressed the regret that he had not read it earlier.[6] Critical theory in this large sense operates by mobilizing concepts and methods that are not necessarily strictly philosophical. But a shared purpose among all these thinkers is to use these concepts and methods in order to call into question the relationship between knowledge or discourse and power. In this sense, criticism has also been understood as a diagnosis of the present and as an engaged practice rather than as a mere theory. Foucault speaks of a "critical ontology of ourselves," which is not to be considered as "a theory, a doctrine, nor even a permanent body of knowledge that is accumulating," but "an attitude, an ethos, a philosophical life in which the critique of what we are is at one and the same time the historical limits that are imposed on us and an experiment with the possibility of going beyond them."[7]

## TWO ATTEMPTS AT RETHINKING AND RELAUNCHING CRITICISM

It is against the background of this complex and multiform heritage that we have to understand the theories of Honneth and Rancière today. Let's specify how they both locate themselves in the tradition of critical theory taken in this broader sense, and how they develop their critical reflections on the unfolding of contemporary social orders.

For Honneth, the Frankfurt School filiation is important and explicitly owned.[8] He also claims other filiations, however, separate from the Frankfurt School but strongly related. The first of these is the Hegelian one,[9] and, in his early writings at least, a Marxian one. Honneth has always been critical toward the "economicist" dimensions of Marxism, but through his early writings at least, he was initially part of the Marxist tradition in a large sense.[10] Moreover, he does not take up the Frankfurt School filiation without criticizing it. He considers the critical tradition as differentiated and multiform.[11] He criticizes some aspects of the research program of the "inner circle" of the first generation of critical theory (the so-called functionalism of this program) while reconnecting with others. Of course, Honneth assumes, above all, a Habermasian filiation, but he also borrows from the first generation of the Frankfurt School and from Horkheimer's interdisciplinary program of research the requirement to link philosophy to the social sciences in order to criticize society as a whole. Honneth's theory of recognition entails this link between social philosophy and the contribution of particular sciences. The theory that the intersubjective relations of recognition, at the affective, legal, and social levels, are the conditions of the constitution of an autonomous subject is both rooted in and extended by research in psychology and psychoanalysis, sociology, the theory of law, the psychopathology of work, and so on.

Let's situate his position more precisely within the field. Honneth continues the tradition of Frankfurt School critical theory particularly insofar as his theory starts from the "social pathologies of reason." These are situations of "social negativity,"[12] out of which a theory of society can counterfactually make explicit the social conditions of a good life. Honneth considers that "the mediation between theory and history," performed notably through a concept of "historically effective reason,"[13] is at the heart of the theoretical identity of the Frankfurt tradition. According to the conception of criticism this school aims to practice, criticism of society must "couple the critique of social injustice with an explanation of the processes that obscure that injustice": this "element of historical explanation" must complement the "normative criticism."[14] Honneth points out the need to theorize the way in which reason is at work in history, in terms of a process of deformation of reason that leads to a neutralization of the normative expectations of citizens, a de-thematization of social injustice in public discussion as a result of which unjust social situations appear as nonproblematic facts. Criticism as he conceives it must neither be abstract or formal nor "give up the normative motif of a rational universal, the idea of a social pathology of reason and the concept of an emancipatory interest."[15]

The need to anchor social critique in forms of rationality that develop throughout history is both what Honneth inherits and what according to him is problematic in the first generation of the Frankfurt School. He considers that the normative standards of criticism remain too implicit in this tradition, and that the concept of social reason as a result is not clarified enough. This is why he takes up the intersubjective and communicative perspective of Habermas, whose main task is precisely to provide such a clarification. Honneth's approach is Habermasian insofar as it is based on the intention to clarify the normative foundations of criticism, in order to avoid a concept of rationality that is too one-sided. He sees such a limited concept at work in Adorno and Horkheimer's famous book *Dialectic of Enlightenment*, as well as in the sociological writings of Adorno. The diagnosis that reason is reduced to a mere instrumental meaning, that it is tightly coupled with domination, brings about damaging confusions in theory as well as in the sociological diagnosis: according to Honneth, it leads to a form of functionalism. According to him, one should give more place to what Habermas calls the life-world, which constitutes a normative resource in the process of reaching an agreement, but also a resistance to forms of domination. Honneth's conception of critique, however, is not strictly Habermasian. Starting with *The Critique of Power*, he attempts to integrate some elements of Foucault's criticism within the Habermasian framework, notably the dimensions of struggle and conflict.[16]

Rancière's approach is critical of the Marxist tradition insofar as it wrongly poses a disjunction between the philosopher and ordinary people. Rancière started with a Marxist and Althusserian approach;[17] in an important seminar, which became a seminal publication, he commented on Marx's *Capital* together with Louis Althusser, Étienne Balibar, Roger Establet, and Pierre Macherey.[18] He then broke with this perspective, accusing it of producing this "epistemological break" between theoretical and everyday perspective. In order to avoid this pitfall, Rancière then took recourse to the archives of working-class discourse ("paroles de la classe ouvrière") to reconstitute political discourses and practices that would make possible a reconfiguration of political space. Discourses and practices are political in the precise sense that they undo the consensus established by the "distribution of the sensible" ("partage du sensible"); they also call into question the link between social position and the capacities attributed to social positions—that is, the capacity to see, say, and determine what is appropriate for such a position. Rejecting some concepts of Marxism, Rancière is therefore not interested in the masses and their practices, but focuses on "the words and fantasies of a few dozen 'non-representative' individuals."[19] This is, in particular, the intention behind *Proletarian Nights: The Workers's Dream in Nineteenth-Century France*, published in 1981. The materials in this study are the "words, reasons, dreams" of a few characters, "a few dozen, a few hundred workers who were twenty years old around 1830 and then resolved, each for himself, to tolerate the intolerable no longer."[20] The "nights" in question are "wrested from the normal sequence of work and sleep," "imperceptible breaks in the ordinary course of things": they were nights "where already the impossible was being prepared, dreamt and seen: the suspension of that ancient hierarchy which subordinates those dedicated to labor to those endowed with the privilege of thought."[21] According to Rancière, it is paradoxically in those nights and writings that "the image and the discourse of working class identity" were "forged," in this paradoxical attempt to tear oneself free from proletarian existence.[22] What he calls a fundamental rejection of the established order is opened here through the constraints of proletarian existence. This attempt at a restitution of workers' voice, far from any reference to class consciousness, is for Rancière the most effective way to undertake the criticism of social divisions that keep everyone in their place.

A paternalistic posture of philosophy is thus attacked by both philosophers, insofar as it is based on a certain inegalitarian logic of emancipation. On this point, Honneth is, like Rancière, skeptical of paternalistic forms of criticism. This appears clearly in his early judgment on Althusser's theory of recognition as ideology, in which Althusser famously accounts for the constitution of subjectivity through the example of the interpellation of a policeman.[23] This, for Honneth, is typically an approach opposed to the one he proposes. According to Honneth, recognition cannot be exclusively ideological, nor can it "subjectivize" totally: insofar as the desire to be recognized can, when injured, reveal the normative expectations of the subjects, recognition provides a potential interpretative framework for social conflicts.

As is clearly illustrated in *The Ignorant Schoolmaster*, Rancière starts from the way criticism is exercised within society. Here he follows the schoolmaster depicted in the book, Jacotot, who bases his teaching on the equality of intelligence.[24] Rancière offers a complete redefinition of what the act of teaching means: it is the ignorant who teaches and produces emancipatory political effects by presupposing equality. What is referred to here and is present throughout the work of Rancière is again a method of equality. The type of criticism that is at stake here is a method of political subversion of the social order. Criticism is not rooted in a genuine subjectivity (as is the case in some readings of Marx or even of Foucault). Critical theory cannot be identified with the scientific account of a posture or a social situation—something Rancière criticizes, in a more or less justified fashion, in Althusser and Bourdieu. Criticism is, for him, an effort to understand an organization of the social, disrupting the positions and challenging the mode of division on which it is based by bringing to light the unrepresented part of society (la "part des sans parts"), the part of those who are not counted and remain voiceless. The concept of the social is thereby redefined. It is not just a concern for power or the outcome of power relations (as is the case in a Foucauldian perspective) or a concern for the truth of politics. The social is rather the result of a division. For Rancière, there are several modes of distributions. One is called the "police," which assigns places and distributes goods; another is called "politics," which refers to the act of contesting this assignment in the name of equality. With such a conception of the social, Rancière therefore proceeds without sociological analyses; indeed, he even questions the epistemology such analyses presuppose. This point opposes him radically to the Frankfurt School tradition.



## TWO DIFFERENT METHODS WITHIN THE CRITICAL TRADITION

The dialogue that took place in Frankfurt thus opposed two different thinkers, who diverge not so much in terms of the critical traditions to which they are attached or the authors to which they refer (Marx, for example), but rather through their methods and their critical approaches to the social and the political. Rancière concentrates on the elements of "disagreement" that hinder all dialogue. The question of the political determination of the community is shifted to another question, that of the scene on which visibility is defined in terms of the difference between noise and speech. In the third chapter of *Disagreement*, Rancière refuses the Habermasian view of the political community as based on the possibility of an ideal agreement. For him, the problem of politics begins where the status of the subject who is able to take part in the community is in question.[25] According to his analysis, every community is originally divided. In chapter 3 of *Disagreement*, Rancière clearly locates his conception of politics, by contrast, with what he thinks is a false dichotomy, between the "enlightenment of rational communication" on the one hand and the "murkiness of inherent violence" or "irreducible difference" on the other, or between the "exchange between partners putting their interests or standards up for discussions" and the "violence of the irrational."[26] It is this identification between political rationality and speech situation that constitutes the presupposition of what should instead, for Rancière, always be in question. Rancière takes the example of the statement "Do you understand?" ("Vous m'avez compris") as the opposite of any performative contradiction. The statement certainly contains an ideal of shared understanding, but on a second reading, it also contains the opposition between people who understand the issues and people who have to understand the orders; therefore, it contains the gap—anchored in logos—between the language of orders and the language of problems.[27]

By contrast, Honneth's theory of recognition continues to work within the Habermasian paradigm of communication. Like

Habermas, Honneth starts from a social experience: not the exercise of communication from which one can draw the presuppositions of the ideal situation, but something that he thinks is more appropriate or even more immanent to social life. It is in terms of the denial of recognition that the conditions for achieving a good life are grasped.[28] Honneth acknowledges and follows partially Habermas's turn from "critique" to "reconstruction,"[29] in which the rules that produce the knowledge and practices of individuals are reconstructed by theory. But Honneth enlarges and corrects the Habermasian framework by taking as his point of departure the negative experiences of being denied recognition and of being treated with contempt in order to bring out the normative expectations, which can become formulated at the affective, legal, and social levels, and which appear damaged or prejudiced in certain configurations of social relations. Thus, if we want the theory to take charge, as Habermas states, of the problems of the people concerned,[30] we must start not from the experiences and structures of communication but from the experiences of injustice that the dominated make and by referencing the language in which they express or fail to express them. From this perspective, it is clear that when individuals want to express the fact that they do not manage to flourish or achieve "self-realization" in existing society, they do not refer to experiences such as pathologies of communication. Honneth considers communication to be irreducible to linguistic exchanges because it has corporeal and broad material dimensions, which necessitate an analysis of the nondiscursive, social signs of contempt and of social invisibility. Honneth therefore inscribes his theory in the continuity of the Habermasian communicative turn, but he also shifts the focus toward recognition to address the shortcomings or deficits of the theory of communication.[31] In the continuity of the normative framework of communicative ethics, his theory broadens and deepens the scope of the conditions of possibility for self-realization by shifting toward the whole array of intersubjective relationships of recognition. He wants to grasp the abstract outlines of communicative reason in a way that has stronger sociological features, searching to anchor it directly in the reproduction of society as a principle of mutual recognition. For Honneth the normative expectations of individuals, which are expectations of recognition, contain a critical potential that can engage a dynamic of social transformation. As a result, criticism for him is the act of bringing to light the normative potential already at work in interactions, the very normative resources that are breached in negative social experiences, and articulating a theoretical framework in which we can do justice to such normative potential.

## A DIALOGUE IN DISAGREEMENT

Given the many divergences between these two different conceptions of the community and their divergent accounts of the possibility of reaching an agreement, how could a dialogue be established? Within the field of the critical tradition broadly conceived, a number of dialogues have already taken place. This plural tradition is crossed by many tensions, some of which have been well visited, while others are not always explicit. We can mention the conversations that already took place between Habermas and Derrida,[32] or between Habermas and feminist thinkers, for instance, around the objections of Carol Gilligan toward Habermas's *ethics of discussion*. Other confrontations marked by misunderstandings and disagreements have occurred, such as Habermas's discussion of the French critical tradition, including Foucault, to whom Habermas famously objected that he did not clarify or make explicit the normative foundations of his critical theory.

Honneth has also engaged in discussions with his contemporaries.[33] His dialogue with Nancy Fraser on the paradigms of recognition and redistribution as a way to rethink social justice[34] is without doubt the most famous, but he also held a very interesting discussion with Joel Whitebook on psychoanalysis.[35] Other, lesser-known discussions have also taken place—for example, with the "sociology of criticism" of Luc Boltanski or the psychodynamics of work of Christophe Dejours.[36] More recent dialogues that have reconfigured the critical field include the important debates between Judith Butler, Ernesto Laclau, and Slavoj Žižek,[37] as well as between Judith Butler and Catherine Malabou.[38]

Apart from those actual dialogues, some important external confrontations—debates on positions reconstructed or even imagined—have also been attempted. Most of them try to establish a dialogue between Habermas and Foucault.[39] This is the case with the interesting book by David Hoy and Thomas McCarthy, *Critical Theory*, which confronts two understandings of the "sueños" of reason (which means either the *dream* or the *sleep* of reason), which, as in Goya's famous etching, produces monsters. The reflection on the historical roots of rationality and argumentation is organized along two divergent views of the "critical" paradigm: a Habermasian one represented by McCarthy, the "continuation-through-processing of the Kantian approach to reason"; and one represented by Hoy, who takes the side of the alternatives offered by Gadamer and Foucault, defending the "contingent character of what counts as rational."[40] I should also mention the book by Ashenden and Owen pursuing the confrontation between Foucault and Habermas in terms of two conceptions of criticism and the Enlightenment (the continuation of Kant's critique and a Foucauldian critique conceived as an ethos), reconstructing the response that Foucault might have given to Habermas's criticism of genealogy. Honneth himself has also made recurrent attempts to set up critical dialogues between his own tradition and a Foucauldian mode of critical thinking. In a number of texts interspersed throughout his career, he has sought to compare Foucault to Habermas, but also to Adorno, insofar as they have in common the commitment to a critique of European reason and they sought to point out the extension of domination that is correlative to the latter's development.[41] Honneth defends Adorno and his idea of a possible reconciliation of subjectivity and its instinctual and imaginary dimensions—dimensions amputated by civilization—against the attack of human subjectivity in general that he believes to be at work in Foucault's writings.[42] In a number of other texts, however, his relationship to Foucault is in fact much closer and he takes to task the Foucauldian legacy. In his early book *Critique of Power*, for instance, he borrows from Foucault an active conception of social struggle. Finally, we can mention the confrontation between Habermas and Derrida, which combines an effective dialogue and the pursuit of an external confrontation in *The Derrida-Habermas Reader*, edited by Lasse Thomassen.[43]

Our *critical encounter* comes under this twofold perspective: it is both a live dialogue and a confrontation that we can carry out a posteriori. It entails a brief dialogue that took place during a meeting in Frankfurt. Like many of the confrontations mentioned above, the confrontation between Honneth and Rancière also intends to be the beginning of an in-depth dialogue: "This dialectical exercise is by no means meant to end discussion on any of the issues raised."[44] The discussion that took place highlights a difference in the theoretical approaches concerning the identification of what is at play in the transformation of society and how such transformation might work, the nature of the social field and its relation to the political, and eventually the very logic of emancipation. It is precisely the differences between Rancière and Honneth that could generate a productive confrontation. By confronting these two influential, divergent critical models, the discussion we propose here and the comparative study we try to initiate highlights in return a number of key aporias that are specific to each thinking but that are also revealed as key stakes in the general project of "critical theory." More specifically, the confrontation highlights the risk that the theory of recognition might lose its political dimension by becoming an exclusively social theory, focusing on the agents as social and not political actors; and conversely the discussion highlights the risk that the theory of disagreement does not sufficiently think its own institutionalization, its own social translation. By doing without the social sciences, without a sufficiently determined view of the social, it runs the risk of overlooking the political issues that are raised from within the social field.

## SOME ANTICIPATED DIFFERENCES

The differences between our two authors, within this complex community of tradition, were readily apparent even before the meeting occurred. Anticipating the encounter, one would hardly expect the presuppositions of each approach to be compatible. As mentioned, in his key work of "political theory," *Disagreement*, as well as in many other texts, Rancière has criticized theoretical approaches focused on the social. For him, the logic of the social is opposed to the logic of the political, insofar as the former rests upon an assignment of positions. The process falling under the concept of government, organizing the gathering of individuals and their consent in a community, is based on a hierarchical distribution of places and functions. As such, it falls outside of politics; it is part of what Rancière famously calls "the police." These assigned positions must be challenged by the assertion of equality, an assertion that takes place through the specifically political act of "subjectivization," which entails a disruption of the unequal relations underpinning the mechanisms and practices of the social sphere. Such a specifically political process is therefore always also a way of "verifying equality."[45] From Rancière's perspective, one could object to a theory of recognition that it presupposes the logic of the social without challenging it, although this is not really the case in Honneth's theory. In the text presented in this volume, "The Method of Equality," Rancière rejects once more the methodological presuppositions of critical approaches, shared by certain forms of Marxism as well as a critical sociology of a Bourdieusian type, that take social inequalities as their starting point and call for a transitional process from apparent inequality to an equality that would be achievable in the future. Rancière therefore proposes nothing less than a redefinition of emancipation: the unequal logic of emancipation, in which the social sciences and critical philosophy play the role of translator of a certain kind of subjectivity and of a relay for emancipatory knowledge (this is the dimension of the ideology critique), is rejected in favor of emancipation conceived as the radical affirmation of equality. In *On the Shores of Politics* in particular, emancipation is defined as the set of practices guided by the presupposition of the equality of anyone with anyone and the will to verify it. Furthermore, the critique of identification is supplemented by a critique of communication. Instead of analyzing, as does Habermas, the procedure that makes it possible for subjects or citizens to reach a consensus, one must question—by insisting on the fundamental dimensions of injustice, on prejudice (*tort*), on the dimension of disagreement or even of the *différend*[46]—the very constitution of the political community and consequently the possibility of communication.

Through these two dimensions—the critique of identification and communication—Rancière's political perspective is linked in a very original way to aesthetics, which is also redefined in the process. Such an aesthetic perspective is not strongly present in the second generation of the Frankfurt School.[47] Rancière indicates on numerous occasions that he intends to reelaborate the meaning of what is referred to as aesthetics. In *The Politics of Aesthetics*, for instance, aesthetics "denotes neither art theory in general nor a theory that would consign art to its effect on sensibility." Rather, it "refers to a specific regime for identifying and reflecting on the arts: a mode of articulation between ways of doing and making, their corresponding forms of visibility and possible ways of thinking about their relationships (which presupposes a certain idea of thought's effectively)."[48] To the extent that the social distribution of places is conceived as a distribution of the sensible, aesthetics redefined in this way has an inherent political dimension. Rancière considers that the division between the visible and the invisible, between what is speech and what is noise, is what is at stake in politics.

Another difference between Honneth and Rancière appears as a result, namely, the emphasis on the moral dimensions of individual and social existence. While normative expectations and moral experience are at the core of Honneth's theory, Rancière criticizes an "ethical turn" in politics and aesthetics, a turn he makes explicit through arguments drawn from the analysis of works of art.[49] For Rancière, the outcome of such a turn is a lack of distinction between fact and law, between being and ought, and the dissolution of the norm into facts. Rancière's analysis of the "ethical turn" does not mean a return to moral standards, but the removal of the division that the very word "morality" involves—the division between law and fact—and finally the transformation of the political community into an ethical community that is supposedly a single substance, made up of one and only people.[50]

According to Honneth, reciprocal recognition is an attempt to establish a positive practical relation to oneself. This does not necessarily mean that we should take a psychologizing approach or that we should refer to a political concept of identity.[51] Honneth relies primarily on concepts and schemes from sociology to reflect on the social conditions of self-realization. Consequently, an approach that is too directly political, one that ignores the successive steps in the institutionalization of normative expectations, as revealed by the theory of recognition, cannot satisfy Honneth. In the last decade, Honneth has turned to Hegel's method in the *Elements of the Philosophy of Right*. The key methodological question he now asks to approach the political is, what type of practices is institutionalized in our societies in such ways that forms of reciprocal recognition are thereby produced and entrenched? Honneth views capitalist societies as institutionalized orders of recognition, and this institutional dimension is increasingly present in his writings.[52] He forges an enlarged concept of justice by bringing out three forms of institutionalization that concern the consideration of the needs of the individuals, their moral autonomy, and the contribution of the individuals to society. There are thus three normative principles that express something about the moral demands that modern individuals can legitimately raise:

the principle of love, of juridical equality, and of performance. Those established principles of modern societies constitute standards for "immanent" social criticism. From this perspective, justice is the outcome of the transformation of the orders of recognition: the result of the back-and-forth movements and tensions between institutionalized principles and unsatisfied claims for recognition expressed by individuals. The notion of justice that is at stake here is far removed from Rancière's revolutionary irruption of equality. Historical evolution demonstrates an expansion of the relations of recognition (the telos of this theory), and criticism proceeds in an immanent way, by articulating the pathologies of society through normative diagnoses, that is, by highlighting gaps between established principles and their actual social realization. Far from being rejected in their content or for their methodologies, the social sciences constitute an essential element in such a critical epistemology. Honneth's concern with the social conditions of self-realization thus hardly seems compatible with Rancière's theory, notably because of the role he confers on social sciences in order to bring out these conditions. The sense of the political is also dramatically shifted: in contrast to an influential model like the theory of Rawls, Honneth continues to raise political questions within the framework of social theory.

Lastly, insofar as the question is also the question of the relevance of critical theory today, we have to specify at least how those forms of criticism are linked to democratic practices. Honneth proceeds to an immanent criticism of the different orders of recognition in our democratic societies; the question of democracy is shifted to the question of the social conditions of possibility for the participation of citizens in the public sphere. For his part, Rancière exercises a radical criticism of the "hatred of democracy," in the name of the democratic principle of the affirmation of a radical equality.[53] For him, democracy refers neither to the form of a representative government, nor to the liberal capitalist society; it is originally a scandal to the hierarchical underpinning of society, namely, the government of the multitude, of those who don't have any title or competence.

## THE DISCUSSION

Let us come back to the live encounter that took place and the actual discussion that we reproduce here, which forms the center of our volume. The discussion is short but touches on central problematics of contemporary social and political theory. The seemingly irreconcilable theoretical differences—which were not totally removed during the exchange—did not impede the discussion, which turned on the central question of the transformation of the existing order. Is the impulse that makes us break with it a need for recognition or rather a desire for equality? The proposed solutions diverged in regard to what we identify as the motor of historical change. The confrontation redefined the question and modified its terms. While Rancière considers the idea of equality to be a presupposition already at work in society, Honneth's perspective leads him to question it in terms of its anthropological presuppositions and to question the hypothesis of an anthropological desire for equality. The theory of recognition also entails a diagnostic dimension, which identifies dissatisfaction with the existing order, or experiences of injustice that are understood in terms of the impact they have on individuals' relationship to themselves. The key normative idea is that individuals can realize themselves only in an order that guarantees the possibility of a good relationship to oneself. If, on the other hand, we take "disagreement" as the point of departure, the affirmation of equality bursts into the social order and produces effects at the moment when we free ourselves from the given identities in order to enact an identity we don't have. In sum, we face two very different approaches, two different methods that seem to exclude each other. Both philosophers endeavored to explain a specific phenomenon: not submission to the existing order, but the overthrow or the subversion of this order. Honneth engages in a subtle analysis of the social, to show that a political transformation of the social is only possible through the struggle for recognition, a struggle that aims to bring about the conditions that are appropriate for the fulfillment of the normative expectations of the subjects. Rancière, in contrast, considers as political an act that makes manifest the tension between subjects that demand equality, on the one hand, and the "policing" (in a broad sense) logics of the social, on the other. He conceives the social as an order of preassigned identities and places.

During the discussion, each philosopher identified something in the other's approach or method that seemed to contradict the critical project of social transformation he purported to defend. Rancière's intervention is based on a critique of the specific conception of the subject and its identity that, according to him, are presupposed by the theory of recognition. He argues that this theory runs the risk of forgetting the moment of disagreement. The struggle for recognition is based on a polemical concept of recognition that entails both a structure of identification and conflict over this identification. But the presence of a different concept of recognition, which presupposes preexisting identities, could vitiate the polemical dimension of this critique. Rancière insists that the demand not to be assigned to an identity must be heard. Taking the first sphere as a case for his demonstration, he argues that the relationship of "love" between mother and baby should actually be thought along a "Proustian model,"[54] which leads to a different conception of identity. To the conception of identity that underlies the theory of recognition, he opposes the idea of "subjectivization" conceived as dis-identification. Moreover, he criticizes the prejudicial implications of the conception of identity at work in the dynamic of recognition: the telos of this dynamic entails the hypothesis of a kind of ethical progress. Rancière puts neither the identity nor the integrity of the person at the core of this dynamic of recognition, but rather equality.

Honneth carried out his own immanent reconstruction of Rancière's theory, based on the second and the third chapters of *Disagreement*. He questions the desire for equality, which drives the process of political transformation in Rancière's theory, and suggests there could be an anthropological given at work here, which Rancière would have to acknowledge. It would be an anthropological given insofar as it is not thought of as taking specific forms depending on the historically changing structures of societies. Honneth attempts to demonstrate that, according to this conception of the political, the transformation of society must be considered as coming under an external critique in Rancière's work—and this leads to a problematic notion of politics. On the one hand, the police order, criticized in an external way, is depicted and thought in a manner that is too rigid for Honneth, as a totally regulated order. Honneth is criticizing here a failure to grasp the complexity of society. The dynamic through which actors reinterpret the normative principles and subvert them is left in the shadows. On the other hand, confining the political to an interruption of the police order does not appear to him as a satisfying way to conceptualize the political, notably from the perspective of the different types of struggles for recognition. Honneth undertakes an immanent critique of the normative principles called into question by actors who feel themselves misrepresented by them and who seek to reinterpret them. Taking up a Hegelian perspective, he considers that the validity of the normative principles of recognition depends on their social effectivity and enforcement. In his most recent work, he takes increasingly as the object of his work the institutional orders of society and the way institutionalized principles of recognition are insufficiently realized.

Two central objections were thus raised. Rancière's critique of Honneth's model of identity asks whether it does not undermine the theory of recognition, and Honneth's critique of Rancière's model of equality asks whether it does not ground an external critique of the political. The German philosopher Christoph Menke initiated the discussion by suggesting that both of these objections rest upon partial misunderstandings of the position of the other. He urged both philosophers to point out which aspects of these objections they could accept. Before coming to any agreement, each reaffirmed what was essential in their theories and what for them remained irretrievably open to criticism in the other's model. Honneth reaffirmed as central the immanence of the critique of the political within social life itself. Rancière maintained that the political is the irruption of equality into the social order, which presupposes a process of "subjectivization" through which the subject must break with pregiven identities.

This debate between Honneth and Rancière thus provided the opportunity to raise a number of significant questions to each of the two approaches: in order to progress in the elucidation of what is a criticism of society, the encounter was the occasion to ask Rancière if there was a place for an analysis of the social in critical theory, and to ask Honneth what the political signification of his conception is. The next two texts, which make the presuppositions of each author explicit, further advanced the understanding of the stakes and difficulties of a contemporary critical theory.

## PRESENTATION OF THE TEXTS

The two texts of Rancière and Honneth presented here are intended to complement the discussion and clarify the theoretical background of each participant. They make it possible to eliminate some objections, while at the same time underscoring their divergences by revealing more clearly the singularities of each position. They are intended to continue the external confrontation of the two authors.

Rancière opposes a "method of equality" to the method of inequality prevalent in critical theory and sociology today. According to this method, equality surges into the social order and enables a political "subjectivization" as discussed above. It is opposed to the constitution of subjectivity as the realization of an identity, even one of personal integrity, as Honneth theorizes it. Rancière is critical of Marxist and even Frankfurt critical theories (he also cites social history and cultural sociology as "discourses of disciplines" that sustain a discourse of competencies), which, according to him, begin with the assumption of inequality and as a result cannot but return to it once again. The explanation of domination and exploitation as coming from the ignorance of the mechanisms underlying social relations leads one in a circle; individuals are dominated because they are ignorant of the laws of domination, and they are ignorant because they are dominated. This kind of explanation inscribes equality in the future—the future of the passage from passivity to activity—that presupposes dissymmetry once again and thus leads back to inequality in the end. Rancière takes aim here at philosophical and sociological methods that operate on the basis of the ancient Platonic identification between social hierarchy and the hierarchy of the souls, and that ground "scientifically" the correlation between social activity and individual, in particular mental, capacities. To this method of inequality, Rancière opposes a method defined as a verification of the presupposition of equality, which consists not merely in aiming for future equality, but in directly producing its effects, precisely by positing it as an "axiom" in the first place. Such a method therefore does not rely on the critique of ideology and illusion (opposing ignorance and knowledge), but rather on the distribution of the sensible and the contestation of the consensus related to the distribution of subjective and social positions.

For Rancière, emancipation is understood as a search for equality that breaks with the actual inequality inherent in social relations. From this perspective, emancipation presupposes precisely a disinterested perspective, which Rancière describes in terms of the Kantian aesthetic judgment. Unlike in a sociological perspective, he doesn't deplore that such idealist judgment forgets social conditions, but views aesthetic judgment as a necessary point of departure for considering things with equality, breaking the link between social occupations and mental equipment. Rancière speaks here of an "aesthetic revolution." Thus, a theorization of political subjectivization that corresponds to a dis-identification largely bypasses the social sciences, and is opposed to the idea of the constitution of autonomy out of preexisting forms of heteronomy, thereby further accentuating the divergence with Honneth.

Against the objections expressed by Rancière, Honneth makes explicit the normative groundings of the realization of integrity.

Already in *The Struggle for Recognition*, Honneth recalled the necessity—related to a "de-substantialized" concept of ethical life (*Sittlichkeit*)[55]—to rethink the historical evolution of modernity toward greater recognition, without anchoring this evolution in the Hegelian metaphysics of the self-realization of the spirit. On the basis of a new interpretation of Hegel, Honneth poses this question afresh and clarifies his immanent conception of criticism. In his essay "Of the Poverty of Our Liberty: The Greatness and Limits of Hegel's Doctrine of Ethical Life," which we are publishing here, Honneth addresses specifically the problem of freedom, which is now the core concept of his normative model. According to him, a differentiated concept of freedom or liberty, one that is adequate to the plurality of the exercises of liberty in our modernity, can only be elaborated in relation to ethical life. Rereading Hegel's *Philosophy of Right*, he shows that in order to fully grasp this concept, we need to insist on the social and institutional foundations of freedom. Individual freedom can only be realized through social institutions, under the condition that the individuals "are equally able to participate in the institutionalized spheres of reciprocity, that is to say in families and personal relations, in the labor market, and in the process of democratic decision-making."[56] By relating to institutions, individuals also relate to themselves since subjective identity is dependent on other-relations for its formation: this is the sense Honneth gives to the Hegelian term "spirit." Spirit is the concept of a reflexive relation to oneself that leads subjects to conceive the objectivity of social reality as a product of the activity of rationally self-relating subjects.

The implication of these analyses is that the concept of liberty can only be fully conceived within the framework of social theory if we want to avoid the "poverty of liberty," as an abstract concept limited to subjective rights and moral autonomy. Honneth wants to elaborate the notion of an objective freedom, embodied in the institutionalized practices. His theory aims at identifying the "general, motivationally formative institutions" that "allow interacting subjects to experience a kind of freedom, that enable each one of their members to recognize in the intentions of the others an objectivity of his own freedom." Those institutions offer a "profound and saturated experience of the absence of constraint." But individual or subjective liberty is not absent: in an institutionalized ethical life, the possibility of retreat and morally articulated protest remains (Honneth quotes Hirschman evoking the famous notions of exit and voice).[57]

Honneth reformulates the relationship between freedom and social theory from his own Hegelian perspective. He accepts the implications of Hegel's idea of a moral progress in history, thereby underscoring once again his distance from Rancière's perspective. Moreover, in making clear that concepts of political theory, such as freedom, can only be clarified from the perspective of a social theory with a normative core, Honneth's text also provides a rejoinder to the political perspective of Rancière.

As counterpoints to the discussion, these two texts clarify the perspectives of each author by highlighting the ways in which they diverge from each other: whereas Rancière defends a political method based on "disagreement," Honneth operates a reconceptualization of the notions of ethical life and freedom. Through this confrontation, the justifiable objections of each thinker to the core positions of the other become apparent. The confrontation thus raises as many problems as it allows us to solve. Must we remain at this point of disagreement, which has moved beyond the state of mere misunderstanding? Do the underlying norms of recognition provide us with the dynamic impulse we need to overcome injustice, or must we look instead to a redefinition of the distribution of the sensible? Do we fall into an illusion of "forced reconciliation" if we search for what unites both critical theories? This volume should help sketch some solid new directions to answer the questions raised by the encounter. It is not only two methods but also two styles that were confronted on the occasion of this philosophical encounter, so that the dialogue is marked by a productive and fruitful distortion. Both authors search for recognition, and both underscore the disagreements and the destabilization of what is common. Our confrontation provides the basis for a future reflection, which has to handle, as one of its leading questions, the imbrication of the social and the political.

two

# BETWEEN HONNETH AND RANCIÈRE

## Problems and Potentials of a Contemporary Critical Theory of Society

JEAN-PHILIPPE DERANTY

THIS PRESENTATION aims to complement Katia Genel's introduction by striving to do two main things: to situate the works of Honneth and Rancière in the broad field of contemporary "critical theory" by studying some of the key conceptual points that define and demarcate these authors' respective positions; and on that basis, to highlight some of the theoretical promises and difficulties harbored by their thoughts. The significant moments these two names represent in contemporary critical philosophy clearly bear the mark of the "traditions" from which their theories have grown. The Honneth/Rancière encounter is thus interesting, among other things, for the new chapter it writes in the complex history that has continuously tied together and opposed "French" and "German" styles of critical theory, ever since something like "French theory" emerged and started to interact with the Frankfurt School tradition.[1] More generally, however, the encounter also reveals some key conceptual parameters of any critical theory project. This is made possible in particular thanks to the substantive points on which Rancière and Honneth actually share germane approaches. The third, more implicit task this presentation sets itself is thus to underline some of the key parameters of a critical theory project.

In the first section, I propose a working definition of "critical theory" to identify the field in which the discussions occur. I try to show that the language of recognition imposes itself quite naturally within the kind of inquiry that can be called "critical theory," even though it is of course not an uncontested manner of speaking. In the following sections, I explore in some detail five important issues I believe the confrontation between Honneth and Rancière raises in particularly interesting ways. First, I focus on some of the issues their discussion evokes regarding the type of "subject-concept" that is required in a critical theory project. I argue that an insufficiently noticed overlap between the two thinkers is their common use of what I call a "hermeneutic of social life," which I contrast with a phenomenology of social life. I then study some of the implications of their rather unique ways of "grounding" their respective critical philosophies. While most contemporary thinkers don't see the need to establish a methodological hierarchy between equality and freedom, Rancière and Honneth are original in making one or the other of those concepts the sole foundation of their social and political thought. Finally, I try to show that the historicism embraced by both Honneth and Rancière might lead them into internal difficulties or lead to shortcomings they might want to avoid.

## CRITICAL THEORY AND THE LANGUAGE OF RECOGNITION

To begin with, we need to give a broad characterization of the field of "critical theory" or "critical philosophy." Several types of philosophical critiques of modern society can be distinguished. The first distinction to be made is between politically conservative and progressive critical theories. Conservative critiques of modern society typically bemoan the demise of authority, or of tradition, or of existing forms of particular institutions, like bourgeois marriage or patriarchal authority, or of the nation-state. Or they adopt a defensive position in relation to existing institutions, like the capitalist markets. Another distinction separates purely conceptual approaches from approaches that use the reference to real existing societies to develop their conceptual core. Some forms of philosophical critique of society remain mainly theoretical in their unfolding, that is, they provide analytical theories of the just or the good in methodological separation from real existing societies and with little or no reference to history, except in the shape of abstract principles like "individual freedom," "modern society," or "liberal-democratic society." In this field, the critical moment consists in measuring the gap between existing society and the norms established by the philosopher. A disciplinary subfield—whether in the form of "social philosophy" or "applied ethics"—is entrusted with the task of establishing the application of the normative theory to empirical social reality. Both in the construction of pure normative theory and in its application, the political assumptions of the theorist are supposed to remain extrinsic to the theoretical work.

In contrast with these two types, Honneth and Rancière are two prominent representatives of another style of critical theory, namely, that field occupied by thinkers working mainly with references in European philosophy who conduct their work on social and political issues in direct connection with real existing social and historical phenomena. In that style of "philosophical critique," theoretical work draws from the empirical realities of social and historical developments; and in turn, one of its main objectives is to provide analytical tools to articulate the criticism of some of these social developments. The substantial methodological connection to social reality and to history distinguishes it from "normative political philosophy." And this form of critical theory can be distinguished from conservative critique because the work of critique is driven by the desire to change society in order to fulfill a universalistic commitment to "emancipation." Emancipation consists in the removal of obstacles to the realization of freedom for all individuals, and is generally viewed as a possibility inherent in modern society, whichever way that possibility is then conceived (as an existing normative principle, a utopian potentiality, a defining ethos, and so on). The negative formulation of the goal of emancipation is significant because it provides this progressive form of theory its inherent critical character, namely, to identify the hurdles to freedom or social justice. Generally, one key obstacle that this kind of critical theory focuses on is characterized in terms of social domination.

The characteristic features of that field explain why the notion of struggle for recognition has strong intuitive appeal within it. On any intuitive understanding of the term, a struggle for recognition names the attempt by a group or a class to "emancipate themselves" from particular oppressive social conditions. And so if the theoretical work elucidates the features of recognition and the struggle waged in its name, it thereby also clarifies the important link just mentioned, namely, the link between theoretical analysis and real existing society. Rancière's initial intervention in the discussion with Honneth shows that there is no problem for him talking about a "Rancièrian theory of recognition." Indeed, he used the concept himself more than ten years before Honneth, in *Althusser's Lesson*.[2] Rancière just disagrees with some of the key concepts used by Honneth in his own theory of recognition. Given the strong prejudice in large tracts of the critical theory field against the language of recognition,[3] it is useful to establish his in-principle agreement.

We get a sense of the place a concept of recognition can take in Rancière's political thinking if we adopt a genealogical perspective and recall the strong link between *Disagreement*, his most systematic book of "critical philosophy," and the archival research he conducted in the 1970s into the first wave of the labor movement in France. It is fair to say that this archival work constitutes the direct source and the constant inspiration behind the arguments presented in *Disagreement*. In *Disagreement* and in all his subsequent political writings, Rancière has constantly returned to the key figures of the labor movement he encountered in this early research. His political ontology appears as a formalization and translation into ontological categories of historical experiences that represent the very paradigm of "struggles for emancipation."

As he was processing this rich historical material, the young Rancière was ineluctably drawn to the language of recognition, for the reasons just stated. The language of "struggles" and "conflicts of recognition" traverses the texts immediately following *Althusser's Lesson*, that is, the introductions to the proletarian texts gathered in *La parole ouvrière* and some of the early texts of *Révoltes logiques* published at the same time.[4] Just as in *Disagreement* twenty years later, the central concept in the texts Rancière wrote to accompany the proletarian texts was the concept of "speech," logos, in the two senses of discursive *reason* and of reason that can *count* as such. Rancière argued that the proletarian struggles revolved around the "question of proletarian dignity."[5] This involved not only demands regarding wages or the organization of the labor process, but just as eminently the demand by the proletarians to have their capacity to speak for themselves "recognized." Proletarian struggle involved "a singular effort of one class to give itself a name, in order to exhibit its situation and respond to the discourse of which it is the object."[6] Already then, Rancière's interpreted Ballanche's reference to the Plebeian retreat to Mount Aventine as "a revolt that is to be identified with the capacity to recognize oneself as a speaking subject and to give oneself a name."[7] These texts from the mid-1970s present arguments that seem fairly close to one of Honneth's earliest texts, "Domination and Moral Struggle," published at about the same time, in which Honneth sought to reinterpret Marx's theory of emancipation as pointing to demands for the recognition of proletarian "dignity."[8] This text directly anticipates Honneth's turn to Hegel in order to find an appropriate, sufficiently complex conceptual grammar, allowing him to explain how political struggles for emancipation can be understood as struggles for dignity.

Similarly, Rancière interpreted the struggle around speech, the struggle to be recognized as having the capacity to speak and for the right to contest the speech of others upon oneself, as a struggle for recognition, as "the desire to be recognized which communicates with the refusal to be despised."[9] Rancière insisted that this effort to be recognized as equal speaking beings was intimately connected to practice, and that "the will to convince the other about one's right entails the resolution to defend it with weapons."[10]

At the time, Rancière analyzed proletarian struggle as a struggle for the recognition of proletarian identity. This early Rancièrian version of the struggle for recognition already exhibited the central conceptual structure of the *litige* as the core issue of politics. Even if the concepts of "subjectivization" or "parts" were not yet in place, Rancière already made the key distinction between a struggle for the recognition of a sociologically or culturally defined identity, which for him was an incorrect interpretation of the workers' aims, and a demand to be recognized in one's identity inasmuch as it underpinned an "equal intelligence." Rancière's interpretation at the time was already that emancipatory politics had a two-stage structure so that the disagreement over the injustice of specific social arrangements implied a more radical, preliminary struggle over the recognition of one's very capacity to take part in dissensus, as a speaking being, a being with logos. Workers, Rancière argued, wanted "to be recognized as something other than the mere strength of numbers and the vigor of working arms; [they aimed] to show that workers can also assert what is just and reasonable, that they have to have their place."[11] What *Disagreement* added later on was a more general argument, in which the worker/bourgeois dichotomy was transformed into the more formal dichotomies of rich/poor and expert/anonymous intelligence. Bourgeois oppression would become *police* in general. But the central idea that the heart of emancipatory politics is the struggle for the recognition of one's capacity to take part in dissensual, polemical conflicts over specific social objects was extracted from the proletarian writings of the nineteenth century.[12]

It is not by chance then that these continue to provide the paradigmatic examples twenty years later, right until today. Indeed, *Disagreement* continues to employ something like a logic of recognition in its most important pages. It does this just as in the earlier text, in the sense of a demand for the recognition of assertions proffered by a speaking being as being valid assertions, in other words, as being assertions proffered by a being whose arguments count, that is, who "can assert what is just and reasonable" and, in that respect, has his or her place in society and therefore deserves a "part" in it.

In our present text, Rancière himself highlights key dimensions of Honneth's model that overlap with his own approach. To begin with, there is the fact that recognition is a social demand, which implies three things. First, it is an expectation on the part of members of society. Honneth would conclude from this that it is a normative claim, but of course Rancière is not comfortable with normative language; in this, he shares the general identification of normativity with oppressive normalization that is characteristic of much contemporary French theory. Second, Rancière agrees with Honneth that this expectation is likely to become more visible, to society and its members, when it is denied, and thereupon in the form of claims for redress, so that demands for justice first emerge as denunciations of injustice. This in turn brings out a third dimension. The demand for recognition stemming from those who are denied it throws a particular retrospective light on the social field, as one that is organized as a particular "recognition order," a specific "*partage du sensible*," in which specific bodies or types of activities or objects cannot be seen and specific voices cannot be heard.[13] Rancière agrees that recognition has "operative" and "antagonistic" dimensions that are important to retain. In turn, these dimensions define politics quite specifically as "struggle for recognition," which can then become broadly synonymous with the *litige* that defines Rancière's politics around the "wrong" that is constitutive of every society. Honneth, just like Rancière, sees no end to the presence of such structural wrong: every *partage du sensible*, or "recognition order," inherently excludes some bodies, voices, or activities as not counting or as not fully counting. Politics is about highlighting, denouncing, and seeking to redress that "tort."

On the basis of this shared commitment to the idea of a struggle against injustice, which in some respects can be interpreted as struggle for recognition, some major disagreements arise between Honneth and Rancière. Studying these disagreements, and the assumptions on which they are based, helps to better understand some of the potentials and limits of contemporary critical theories of society.



## THE HERMENEUTIC AND PHENOMENOLOGY OF SOCIAL EXPERIENCE

In Rancière's initial account, the dissensus that is constitutive of politics was articulated in reference to the denial of specific identities, more specifically, proletarian identity. In his mature version, the concept of "identity" becomes negatively loaded as a category belonging to the grammar of the police order, the very grammar that political dissensus seeks to challenge. Rancière famously contrasts "identity," as a marker of social belonging, with a formal or empty concept of "subject," as the outcome of a political process of "subjectivization." Subjecthood is defined in a way that recalls the earlier structuralist emphasis on the Marxist concept of "support," as a mere function or ontological place holder in a structural field, defined independently of any essential traits.[14] This "structural" or "ontological" notion of subjecthood is one feature in which Rancière's training in structuralist Marxism can still be traced.

However, in the context of the confrontation with Honneth, Rancière in fact objects to the notion of "identity" for the very purpose of developing an adequate theory of recognition. He does not make the mistake of confusing Honneth's notion of identity with the meaning the concept has in debates in multiculturalism. Indeed, Rancière's carefulness in this regard points to another overlap, namely, that for the two authors the political process, the struggle for recognition in Honneth and the process of subjectivization in Rancière, contains a key performative power whereby the political subject is transformed by, and in a sense is born out of, the political process.

Nevertheless, even if Rancière acknowledges the plasticity and the dynamic dimensions of Honneth's concept of identity, it is at this point that he finds the most to object to. Rancière's criticism is immanent to the problem of recognition: grounding the model of recognition in the norms of personal identity makes the very project of recognition politics untenable. If recognition is to be "operative," it has to challenge the existing order, since politics is about creating "an original configuration of the world."[15] And if that is to happen, then in turn the struggle for recognition cannot be about re-cognizing stable identities, whether those are already fixed, as in a multiculturalist version, or whether those are postulated as the telos of recognition, as in Honneth's model. I note that these two forms of recognition, which struggle against social contempt (the classical multiculturalist concern for minority identities and the Honnethian struggle for full personal identity), can be well conceptualized in Rancièrian terms, provided that their description is altered. They should be analyzed as struggles for a new configuration of the common world in which particular bodies, voices, sites, objects, which so far have been excluded from the realm of collective deliberation, become sites and objects for such deliberation.

Identity and subjecthood are two different conceptual approaches to subjectivity as critical theories need to include them within their general models. Such subject-concepts are indispensable in many models of critical theory because they are centrally implicated at the different interlocked levels at which these models seek to intervene: at the level of the (more or less developed) theory of society implied by the critical theory; at the level of its implications for political theory, through its (more or less explicit) conception of political agency; in its (more or less explicit) conception of social movements; and of course in its account of social pathologies, or injustice, and their effect on individuals and groups, which usually links up in some way with the previous two levels.[16]

Given his anti-phenomenological orientation, Rancière's own brand of critical theory does not operate through the interlinking of levels just suggested. In Rancière's theory, the subject-concept is there only to specify the kind of agency at play in political action. Given that politics for him is a radical rupture of the police order, the subject-concept must relate only to the political moment. Therefore it does not communicate with other dimensions of subjectivity, such as the sociological or psychological ones. Honneth's critical theory, by contrast, adheres fully to the suggested layering in separate but connected levels around a central subject-category. In his writings preceding *Freedom's Right* at least, personal identity is a subject-concept that plays a role not just in the political-theory side of theory, but also at the descriptive level, in the diagnosis of social pathologies, and at the normative level. Despite clear differences on this point, however, a significant point of contact exists between Honneth and Rancière in relation to this subject-pole of critical theory. Both make a strong appeal in their methods to what might be called the hermeneutic of social experience.[17] This common reference to social experience as having epistemic value contrasts with their diverging attitudes toward what I will call the phenomenology of social life.

Honneth's use of a substantive notion of subjectivity in his early and middle periods is a trademark of the post-Hegelian tradition of critical philosophy. This tradition arguably starts with Hegel himself since his theory of "subjective spirit" proposes a rich anthropological model of human freedom, the "subjective" counterpart and indeed in a sense the platform for what the theory of "objective spirit" exposes at the legal, social, and political-institutional levels. Hegel's direct successors, Feuerbach and Marx, did not latch explicitly onto Hegel's anthropology but retained Hegel's core idea of "concrete freedom," which they sought to develop in materialist and naturalist terms. This tradition was pursued by the different "generations" of Frankfurt School critical theory, all the way to Honneth.[18] What characterizes this legacy is the way in which thick conceptions of subjectivity are integrated at different levels of the theoretical edifice.[19] These thick theories of subjectivity are developed as philosophical anthropologies, and provide important planks in normative frameworks, from the mimetically integrated subject in Adorno, to the subject in communication for Habermas, to Honneth's autonomous subject. In each case, the normative anthropology also provides key elements for the critical, diagnostic side of the theory, both at the conceptual level, in accounts of key concepts such as alienation, reification, and ideological obfuscation, and at the empirical level, in applications of the model to real social phenomena.

After the initial critical reception of his major book, Honneth gradually shifted on the understanding of identity. The subject-concept at the heart of the theory of recognition changed in ways that were not insignificant. In recent years, culminating in his major new work, *Freedom's Right*, Honneth has largely abandoned the anthropological grounding of his theory of justice and reinterpreted the fundamental norm of individual autonomy in a historicist and social-theoretical perspective. Autonomy is now considered mainly as a moral achievement of modernity and thereby as secured by modern society's core institutions. Recognition now names the structure of reciprocal expectations that bind subjects in social life and that represent the conditions for the realization of their intermeshed individual goals. In order to reach individual aims that realize key dimensions of their autonomy, each social subject has to assume that there are others who share with him a similar normative attitude, so that it is only by recognizing one another in that capacity that these interlocked individual goals can be realized. This logic is true for friends, participants in the market, and citizens in the public sphere. The institutions of modernity define modes of social behavior and social roles, which, when endorsed by subjects, allow them to engage in the kind of social action that makes possible the realization of their goals. Recognition therefore continues to play the role of the condition of autonomy, and as a consequence it remains the normative foundation of the model, but its psychological meaning is no longer decisive. Instead, recognition now points to reciprocal expectations that are equally social and functional (without recognition, some key types of social action are impossible) and normative (these forms of social action are conditions of freedom). In this new model, moral expectations linked to reciprocal forms of recognition now constitute a screen, as it were, between the agents' psychic worlds and social structures. Recognition has become a moral concept in an institutional sense; it is an "ethical" concept, in the Hegelian acceptation of the term. The basic assumption of a need for autonomy provides the ultimate motivational foundation but it is no longer sufficient by itself to delineate the content of modern struggles for emancipation.

In one important respect, there is still a continuity between Honneth's earlier writings and his new model, namely, the epistemic role played by social and historical experience. Whether recognition is defined anthropologically, as in the earlier writings, or institutionally, as in the new model, a significant implication in all cases is that the social experiences of modern subjects have irreplaceable truth-value. That is, subjective expectations, the normative expectations that are expressed and conceptualized from the point of view of the subjects, when considered from a broad enough perspective (across populations or across time), point to norms that have a significant purchase in reality. These norms form the social glue that helps to account for social reproduction at the level of social theory or social ontology. They are the ground for negative experiences explaining struggles for recognition (the model of social movements in *The Struggle for Recognition*) or explaining political movements arising from the malfunctions of core institutions (as in *Freedom's Right*). And it is by appeal to these norms that a diagnosis of social pathology can be developed. At these different levels, subjective experiences of social life thus provide a decisive theoretical guideline, so that critical theory needs to encompass an important hermeneutic moment, what we might call a hermeneutic of social experience. In building his or her critical social theory, the theorist can trust—in fact it is one of the theorist's main tasks to do justice to—the contents of social experience and their historical transformations. Critical theory, on this account, has to provide the conceptual vocabulary that will capture the truth-content of historically significant expressions of social experience. Indeed, we should speak of two distinct hermeneutic elements within critical theory: a hermeneutic of social experience undertaken from a synchronic perspective, which represents a form of social ontology rooted in empirical social and historical knowledge;[20] and a hermeneutic of historical experience, which implies a diachronic perspective, inasmuch as historical transformations leave their mark on subjective experience and subjects and collectives refer to historical achievements and historical experiences in making normative claims.[21]

The shift to an institutional, "social-ontological" sense of recognition in Honneth's recent writings leads to a relative severing of the link between experience and critique, a distancing from phenomenology, if by that we simply designate the whole content of individual experience.[22] In the earlier model, the concept of recognition was used simultaneously in phenomenological and normative ways. This multifold aspect of recognition ensured that there was, in principle, overlap between the breadth of negative forms of social experience typical of a given society and the conceptual tools used by the critical theory. In this methodological setup, critical theory could seek to do justice to the full gamut of physical and psychic injuries caused by social structures; it therefore did not just contain a hermeneutic element, looking at social structures from the point of view of subjective actions and expectations, but it could also set for itself the goal of being the representative in theory of the phenomenology of social suffering.[23] With the shift to an institutional concept of recognition, the overlap between the hermeneutic and the phenomenological tasks is no longer in place. Injustices and pathologies of recognition are now conceptualized as breaches of moral promises, namely, the promises of social freedom contained in key social institutions. To take the example of modern labor, it is telling that Honneth approaches injustices and pathologies of modern work solely from the perspective of how they contravene the expectations that underpin individuals' participation in the labor market as an institution. The phenomenology of unjust or exploitative or alienating work practices falls out of the purview of the new framework. Honneth still refers empirically to pathologies of work, but their significance is only indirect: they matter as *indices* of a failure in regards to a moral promise, failures that can be read off hermeneutically in terms of claims and expectations, but that are no longer significant in and of themselves, for what they *actually* do to people.

The position Honneth now defends is, in some limited respects, comparable to the one advocated by Rancière, namely, to the extent that both reject full-fledged phenomenological perspectives on social and political issues, but make room for the hermeneutic dimension in another respect. They include this element to the extent that they consider that their social hermeneutics give conceptual shape to the claims made by individuals and groups, and thereby also presume these claims to be epistemically valid. The norms involved in those claims and the manner in which they are endorsed and interpreted by these theories obviously differ: individual freedom for Honneth, equality for Rancière; normative reconstruction versus equality of intelligence. But for Rancière as for Honneth, a key aspect of theory is that it makes room for the actual demands of individuals and groups without distorting, suspecting, or rejecting them, indeed taking them as epistemic and practical guidelines.

By contrast with Honneth, there has always been a notable absence of any reference to the thick "content" of subjecthood, any appeal to psychological reality or phenomenological arguments, in Rancière's writings. We can note that the tradition in which his work is commonly located, that is, the "post-structuralist" field, is affected by a particular kind of ambiguity in this respect. Poststructuralism borrows some of its most defining traits from the seminal work of Althusser. Among other things, it inherits from Althusser a dismissive attitude toward phenomenological arguments. It is no coincidence that the return to Althusser that is advocated today by a number of writers working within the poststructuralist tradition is often framed in terms of a battle "contra phenomenology" or to announce "the end of phenomenology."[24] The paradox is that the Lacanian reference is also a defining one in this post-Althusserian field.[25] Indeed, the most illustrious contemporary critical theorists in that camp, thinkers such as Butler, Žižek, Laclau, or Mouffe, make reference to highly elaborate models of the psyche, usually Lacanian or at least "post-Freudian," to ground their social and political theories.[26] Indeed, despite his decisive rejection of the content of subjective experience as having any relevance in any aspect of philosophical work, Badiou has consistently developed his formal ontology in reference to Lacan.[27] Assuming that "poststructuralist" critical theory forms a minimally homogeneous field (which it does institutionally), how is it possible to accommodate the extensive use of thick models of subjectivity, including psychoanalytical ones, while maintaining an anti-psychological and an anti-phenomenological stance? The answer to this conundrum seems to lie in two related assumptions of poststructuralist approaches, which are directly inherited from Lacan and Althusser, namely, that the individual desires are wholly shaped in their mediation through language; and that the social constitution of language makes the subject wholly dependent upon the overarching symbolic order as a result. Radical social constructivism, itself based on a discursivist conception of ontogenesis, makes it possible simultaneously to reject psychological and phenomenological arguments and to refer to thick theories of the human psyche, notably to psychoanalytical schemes, for social and political critique.

Rancière's anti-psychologism is close to theories with a poststructuralist bent in that respect. In particular, he shares with poststructuralist thinkers the rejection of what he calls with disdain the reference to "flesh and blood,"[28] that is, any reference to the somatic or affective dimensions of subjectivity as explanatory or diagnostic principles. Here, we should note in passing that Feuerbach has remained an odd, minor paradigmatic figure for Rancière, in a negative sense.[29] But Rancière is squarely at odds with poststructuralist thinkers in relation to the hermeneutic of social experience. A defining Althusserian gesture that can be identified in numerous versions throughout poststructuralist writings, a gesture explicitly associated with Lacan's own reappropriation of Freud, consists in describing the subject as a surface phenomenon produced by a structure that functions as an "absent cause." A key methodological implication of this approach is that the many structural factors responsible for the content of subjectivity cannot be accessed by it, making the subject constitutively "mystified."[30] Such thick accounts of subjectivity therefore also provide—indeed they define as their major theoretical goal the ability to provide—an explanation as to why a hermeneutic of social experience not only cannot be trusted, but in fact is to be essentially distrusted. It is this very consequence that is at the heart of Rancière's rupture with Althusserianism. The core Rancièrian objection to Althusserianism is precisely that the radical distrust of people's voices and practices leads to theoretical and political elitism, which in the end reproduces the domination and social segregation it allegedly seeks to combat. Rancière defends the reference to experience in his anti-Althusserian charge, to the extent that human beings are speaking beings that can articulate their claims and organize and describe their own practices.[31] This combination of antielitism and anti-psychologism leads him to take up a position that is precarious, since it is difficult to see how one can dissociate claims from the experience that these claims arise from, hermeneutics from phenomenology. Political claims arguably arise as claims *about* aspects of social reality, and since the claims are to be made by the agents themselves, some anchoring of politics within forms of experience appears inevitable. It is revealing that in passages in which the contentful aspect of recognition claims comes to the fore, Rancière names the social agents with the equivocal phrase of "speaking bodies," a term that acknowledges and hides their "flesh" in the same movement.[32]

The conclusion that can be drawn from these parallel analyses is that Rancière's constructivist conception of the political subject leads to a position that is, in some limited sense, comparable to Honneth's institutionalist, social-theoretic turn in relation to the "subject of critical theory." Both share the conviction that it is the role of theory to be attentive to the content of social experience, notably as it asserts itself historically.[33] An important dimension of critical theory for them is to document and echo at the conceptual level the content of social expressions, notably the forms of the demands for emancipation, as they have manifested themselves through history. Similarly, both believe that it is not the role of critical theory to represent the full phenomenology of social suffering in theory. For both thinkers, social critique concerns contradictions within, or indeed *of*, the universal, and politics denotes a collective struggle to denounce and redress those contradictions inherent in the universal. Rancière's argument that "anyone" can make themselves the political subject endorsing the struggle for recognition around a particular "tort" makes it perfectly clear that there is a disconnect between the actuality of a particular experience of injustice and the political demands arising from those experiences. Political struggle, for Rancière, is waged not over a specific form of social injustice, but rather at the second-order level of the capacity of subjects to be heard about that injustice. Ironically, such an emphasis on the discursive aspects of political struggle bears some resemblance with a proceduralist move of the kind Habermas advocated. Rancière famously expressed his disagreement with Habermas for assuming that the stage of communication is always already in place when in fact it is the very existence of such a space that is at stake in politics.[34] And yet the distance that Rancière's model instigates between suffering and injustice, on the one hand, and the contested access to representation and the space of reasons, on the other, is typically one also propounded by Habermas. Rancière's conception of politics thus oddly but arguably resonates with the core insights of post-Habermasian models like those of Nancy Fraser, who makes "participatory parity" the core norm of critical theory, or the model developed by Rainer Forst, for whom the point of justice and of struggles against injustice is the right of individuals to have their voices count as expressions of reason and is, as a result, their demand to be treated as agents to whom reasons are due.[35]

One final remark is worth making in comparing the place and structure of subject-concepts in the critical theories of Rancière and Honneth. However paradoxical this might sound, it could be argued that their intellectual trajectories in relation to the phenomenological, "somatic" moment in critical theory are in fact running in opposite directions. In his early writings up to and including *The Struggle for Recognition*, Honneth sought to ground critical theory anthropologically, in a thick concept of self-realization with strong psychological traits. One aspect of this move was a deliberate critical stance toward Habermas, precisely on the question of the theoretical articulation of negative social experiences. The theory of recognition was developed notably in order to correct what the young Honneth perceived as the danger of overrationalization contained in Habermas's grounding of critical theory in communication. One of the main points of the first theory of recognition was to allow a distinction to be made between the normative validity of claims of injustice based on an actual experience of injustice and the validity of the public expression of those claims.

For the young Honneth, Habermas's proceduralism, in defining normativity, ran the risk of collapsing the difference between the justification of the content of claims and the justification of the mode in which claims are made.[36] The thick concept of self-realization was meant precisely to allow for the whole content of the nondiscursive in social experience (that is, affective and psychological states and embodied modes of social experiences), to receive its full place in the critical enterprise, not only at the descriptive level, but also in the normative grounding of critique. Increasingly however, Honneth has distanced himself from his early criticisms and has realigned his position with Habermas. He now agrees with Habermas about the need for normative claims to be universalizable so they can count as rightful claims.[37] This comes across in our text when he now agrees with Rancière that the experience of suffering is not sufficient to ground by itself a valid political claim.

By contrast, in the shift from the historiography of the labor movement to the historiography of modern aesthetics, Rancière has reintegrated, in a certain sense, the somatic and the prediscursive, with direct implications for politics. In many passages in his aesthetic writings, Rancière seems to reinvest his subjects with an organic constitution; the "flesh" makes a reappearance at the heart of the theoretical exercise. This becomes particularly striking in *Aisthesis*, which extends the aesthetic framework developed over the last two decades into performance and minor art forms. The book can be read in part as a nonexhaustive study into the types of bodies that the modern regime of perception makes not only aesthetically possible but also politically relevant, from the fragmented, to the automated, to the passive body. At first, such an aesthetic taxonomy does not seem to bear on the social and the political. But the aesthetic and the political are intrinsically linked in Rancière. The aesthetic is inherently political since creative and artistic practices (which for him are not restricted to the high arts) are foremost in questioning an extant "sharing of the sensible."

In fact, read from this aesthetic perspective, the central notion of the "sharing of the sensible" introduced in *Disagreement* takes on an irrepressible phenomenological dimension. Rancière thinks of social orders as structures in which the perception of and value attributed to "ways of doing, being and speaking" are socially framed and thus socially predetermined. The police is the institutional order that operates on the basis of, and in turn constantly reinstates, such sharing and distributing of what is socially perceptible. The mode of operation of the police thus intervenes directly in perception; it is a form of *aisthesis*. Rancière defines it as "a distribution of bodies according to their visibility and invisibility,"[38] and as "the system of a priori forms determining what presents itself to sense experience."[39] The terminology is unmistakably "transcendental." Since the police designates the (socially produced) "a priori" conditions of perception and indeed anchors them in socially validated bodies, it can rightly be called phenomenological, in the technical sense of the term this time.

Politics, for Rancière, is the attempt to challenge this police-*aisthesis* and to construct another one, in other words, to install an alternative way to "count" bodies, parts, and their shares. But there are two possible ways to challenge a prevailing *aisthesis*. In *Disagreement*, the political contestation of the *partage* at the heart of the police order is mostly a discursive exercise, the contesting through argumentation of the exclusions from the common "stage." To use Forst's central concept, politics in *Disagreement* is a battle of justifications, mainly a battle about what counts as justification and who is entitled to proffer and expect justifications. In the later aesthetic writings, however, the emphasis shifts away from the exclusive agonism of logos, and the modes of contestation of the *partages du sensible* become more varied. In *Aisthesis* Rancière makes a concerted effort to highlight new modes of bodily activity and indeed new modalities of affectivity, made possible by the modern aesthetic regime, to present them as new modes of contestation of the a priori forms of experience that are consonant with bourgeois domination. The anarchistic bodies of clowns, the passive body of Julien Sorel, the automatic body of Charles Chaplin take on a revolutionary charge as they undermine the existing, hierarchical distribution of the sensible.

Even if the reference to these bodies is not psychological or anthropological, it takes Rancière's framework well outside the poststructuralist model. The bodies in Rancière's late work escape totalizing discursive and symbolic overdetermination; this is precisely what makes them rebellious bodies. Bodies in these writings enact an anarchistic principle: they literally embody radical equality by just being bodies that show, through their activities and indeed at times through their utter passivity, their resistance to "the big Other" of the *partage du sensible*, the capacity to escape social overdetermination. *Aisthesis* in many passages reads like a modernist illustration of Spinoza's famous dictum—"nobody knows what a body is capable of"—and appears to elevate this to one of the privileged ways in which the utter contingency of every social "*arkhe*" can be questioned.

## AUTONOMY AS FOUNDATIONAL NORM

Rancière resists Honneth's grounding of critique and politics in the psychologically loaded concepts of integrity and identity. But these two concepts for Honneth are simply synonymous with autonomy or, even more simply, with freedom. Instead, Rancière wants to ground critique in the concept of equality. The discussion between the two philosophers regarding the correct concepts to use in order to "ground critique" is especially revealing of the underlying defining assumptions of each of their positions. It also points to a crucial element in any critical theory project more generally, namely, the "foundational" principle or norm that is to underpin such a project.

To begin with, it should be noted how striking it is that the confrontation between the two philosophers opens up such an alternative between equality and freedom. Radical-democratic conceptions of politics usually hold the two concepts together; indeed, the tension in their "co-originarity" is commonly an important aspect of a critical theory's specific contribution.[40] Such irreducibility holds not just for the European radical-democratic tradition, but also for much Anglo-American political philosophy, whether in liberal versions of egalitarianism,[41] or radical versions of egalitarianism,[42] or indeed for the capability approach.[43] The same is also true for the many contemporary theorists inspired by Hannah Arendt, for whom political freedom both entails and realizes the equality of social participants.[44] For most critical theorists, the irreducibility and co-originarity of the norms of equality and freedom are accepted as a basic assumption about modern society.

Honneth's resistance toward equality as the foundational norm is twofold: it entails a conceptual and a methodological moment.

For Honneth, equality and liberty are not co-originary because demands for equality in fact only express some of the dimensions of a claim that is more fundamentally expressed as the need for autonomy, understood as the capacity for self-realization. Equality therefore has its place in Honneth's thought, but is not sufficient to ground itself, as it were. It is interpreted by him as a particular way of cashing out the norm that is the one subjects really intend, namely, personal freedom in its multiple dimensions.

This "downgrading" of equality in terms of normative primacy occurs already in the writings of his middle period around *The Struggle for Recognition* and in the debate with Fraser. Equality in this first model is a valid norm in the second sphere of recognition; it distinguishes the status of modern individuals inasmuch as each and every one is to be considered worthy of respect. It is typically a normative status arising with modernity, linked to the horizontal universality of all agents. It articulates the fact that each and every individual has to be considered morally responsible and, to that extent, equally entitled to contribute to collective legislation, whether in a moral sense, in the constitution of a kingdom of ends, or in political terms, as a participant in citizenship. But in Honneth's construct, this particular sense of equality only enacts specific dimensions of freedom as autonomy: in particular, the equality of status that is at stake here is a condition for freedom of conscience and civic freedom. Honneth makes full room for this egalitarian moment; indeed, he often highlights the importance of this norm by comparison with others. But the norm of equality is not placed at the same conceptual level as freedom precisely because Honneth defines freedom in a perfectionist way. Equality of status only makes explicit one of the senses in which modern individuals can be free and consequently one of the normative demands they're entitled to make.

Equality in a distributive sense already comes into play in that second sphere as one of the ways in which equality of status translates into social rights, notably the social rights of full citizens.[45] Finally, equality in a distributive sense arises a second time, this time in the third sphere of recognition, inasmuch as the demand for esteem recognition translates into the claims for a fair distribution of social goods as they relate to contributions to social cooperation. Here, Honneth reinterprets "geometrical" equality, an equality that can be unequal but fair inasmuch as it ensures that everyone receives their due in proportion to their specific contribution to social life. In these three senses, the different types of equality make explicit particular dimensions of the singular need or demand for self-realization. Equality in each case is grounded in liberty.

In *Freedom's Right*, Honneth makes the conceptual primacy of freedom over equality even more explicit and basic. As he writes forcefully at the start:

> I do not address the notion of "equality," as influential and consequential as it might be, as an independent value because it can only be understood as an elucidation of the value of individual freedom, as the notion that all members of modern societies are equally entitled to freedom. Everything that can be said about the demand for social equality only makes sense in relation to individual freedom.[46]

Equality can be a normative claim only on the basis of the more fundamental claim arising in modernity, that *all* must be able to be free. The content of equality does not matter in this respect. Equality only comes into play as a *universal* demand, and the normative justification for this universality is the Hegelian requisite that "all must be free." The universality of full freedom (autonomy), in all of its different articulations, is the core of any demand for equality.

Recent writings make explicit another set of arguments that were always in the background, namely, a polemical attack on the "distributionist" paradigm in political philosophy.[47] From this perspective, it becomes problematic to make equality a primary norm, as this often leads to a misleading approach in political theory, one that conceives of the subject as an atomic entity that can survey its own goods as possessions and to whom primary goods are to be equally distributed as possessions. In this case, Honneth's qualm about equality as a primary norm is that it misdescribes what justice is about. Justice from his neo-Hegelian perspective is not primarily about the fair distribution or redistribution of social goods, but about equal access to the conditions of self-realization. Equality does feature there, but in a variety of meanings, not all reducible to distribution. And once again, the conceptual work is done by freedom and the universality imperative. To make distribution, or redistribution, the driving methodological tool, or to express the problem of justice in the grammar of distribution, is to put the theory on the wrong track. And as Honneth asserts, such inadequate conceptual grammar is directly responsible for the disconnection between political philosophy and political reality.

Honneth's favoring of liberty over equality is of course different from the way in which mainstream political liberalism makes liberty the prime value, lexically preceding considerations of fair distribution or redistribution. This substantial difference relates to the different conceptions of freedom at play in the liberal tradition and in the tradition from which Honneth's philosophy emerges. Honneth's concept of freedom, as recalled, is a perfectionist one.[48] It is defined by reference to the telos of a state of unhindered individual flourishing resulting from ideal supporting social conditions. We might call it Aristotelian based on the current carving up of the theoretical field in contemporary ethics, but of course this strong perfectionism does not take its roots in Aristotle, but rather in the post-Hegelian heritage, in the tradition stemming from Feuerbach and an anthropologically read Marx, all the way to first-generation critical theory. Placing Honneth's philosophy in the intellectual tradition from which it emerges is useful because it immediately makes clear what theoretical benefits it is hoped can be drawn from such a strong perfectionist approach in social and political philosophy. The strong perfectionism of the post-Hegelian scene allows theorists to tie normative considerations in moral and political philosophy, with substantive considerations about subjectivity and society. From this perfectionist perspective, it makes sense to favor freedom over equality as the most fundamental norm. Equality is indeed something that can be demanded. As we saw, there is no debate about its importance in real moral and political conflicts. But equality arises as a demand only for beings whose core interest lies elsewhere, namely, in the integrity of their own person. There are two meanings of "justice" from this perspective: a general one, whereby justice is the universal ideal condition allowing for the flourishing of each and every person; and specific senses of justice that spell out the different ways in which that universal demand can be more specifically cashed out in the institutional complexity of social life. Indeed, as Marx's polemic against equality in the *Critique of the Gotha Program* indicates, equality can even be a dubious or ambiguous norm for emancipatory politics. In this polemic Marx directly anticipates the complex intricacies that arise as soon as a theory of justice is defined in terms of the correct method for devising fair distribution or redistribution. By contrast, the principle of maximum individual flourishing puts a clear constraint on the rule of equality, thereby proving the methodological primacy of freedom over equality.

Another significant aspect is the scope of social transformation that a particular political-theory paradigm countenances as a result of its very theoretical setup. The emphasis on social relations underpinning the conditions of individual freedom and the consonant rejection of the distributionist and proceduralist paradigms do not necessarily amount to a more "radical" agenda, but at the very least they stem from a more radical tradition of political thinking. This is the tradition within political philosophy, with Marx as its main proponent, which considers that it is insufficient in practical terms and theoretically wrong-headed to consider issues in politics independent of the modality of social relations. Because in this tradition a close connection is established between politics and social relations, a third core value next to freedom and equality also arises as part of the normative fundament, namely, the value of solidarity. Again, this core value runs through the tradition from which Honneth's model has grown. Honneth explicitly retrieves Hegelian *Sittlichkeit* in this sense,[49] but the value of solidarity, that is, the requisite of reciprocal support and its attendant practical consequences between coparticipants in society, is also a fundamental value in pre-Marxist socialist and Marxist politics.[50]

Honneth's critical perspective on the distributionist approach in political philosophy is shared by a number of other critical theorists.[51] However, in these other models, freedom and equality are presented as equally important norms, neither of which is reducible to the other. By contrast, the primacy of freedom advocated by Honneth stands out. This appears most strikingly by contrast with the model elaborated by David Miller in *Principles of Social Justice*. Even though Miller's writings do not exactly fit within the "critical theory" field as it was vaguely defined at the start, reference to his model is still appropriate since, as Honneth himself has noted, Miller's theory of justice overlaps with Honneth's in substantive ways.[52] Miller argues, like Honneth, that the norms of justice are to be reconstructed empirically from specific types of social interaction. And he lists three spheres of justice that overlap very well with Honneth's spheres of recognition. Miller, however, contrasts two independent concepts of equality. The second, social equality, corresponds to the kind of equality Honneth considers a dimension of the social conditions enabling individual freedom. But Miller argues strongly that another, independent concept of equality needs to be distinguished from social equality, namely, equality as distributive justice, equality as receiving what one is due. Using Miller as a germane reference helps us to raise skeptical questions in relation to Honneth's downgrading of equality: Is justice understood simply as the demand to receive what you are due (whether in material or symbolic terms) soluble in freedom? Is justice in this sense only something people request *in order to* achieve or assert their freedom or does the norm have authority *on its own*? Can't individuals be free and yet suffer from an unjust distribution or redistribution? Are struggles for distributive justice always to be interpreted as struggles for (the conditions of) freedom?

For other critics of distributionist approaches such as Rainer Forst, these questions do not raise any specific problem because the fundamental norm they use is not perfectionist autonomy, but individual dignity, whose political significance is cashed out in terms of a right to justification. From that perspective, the distinction between social equality and distributive equality can be retained but the two concepts can be hypostatized under the more fundamental demand to be treated equally as a being to whom justification and the capacity to engage in justificatory practices are due. Distributive justice from this point of view is just one aspect of the social practices about which justificatory procedures are to be put in place.

For Honneth, however, the independence of distributive equality from social equality is a problem. We are so used to thinking about a human being's moral status in Kantian terms that we struggle to understand the assertion of that moral status, which translates into the idea that justice is due to that being, in terms other than the recognition of that being's capacity for autonomy. Honneth's account of distributive equality through the second and third spheres of recognition rehearses that Kantian background. But Miller's case for an analytical distinction between distributive and social equality and Rancière's formal, "ontological" defense of equality both suggest in different ways that it is possible to question this link between equality and freedom, which reduces the demand for equality to an aspect of autonomy. It is conceivable that equality has its own normative authority, independently, in some cases at least, of the recognition of autonomy. If that were true, it would simply be a primitive meaning of justice, independent of the recognition of one's freedom, to demand to receive one's due. There might be many possible links between the two norms, but it is conceivable that two interrelated core meanings of justice are simply: to "receive what you are due" and "to give to others what they are due and nothing more." Indeed, against the dualism of meanings of justice presented by Miller, one could argue that it is in fact distributive equality that constitutes the core sense of justice. This would be distributive equality no longer understood in an economist, or "distributionist," sense, but understood "social-ontologically," as the demand expressed by each and every person that they should receive what they are due and should give to others only what others are due.

This question is inherently linked to the problem of historicism. The Kantian assumption regarding the analytical link between equality and freedom functions particularly well in a modernist framework, in which the demand for equal treatment can be presented as one dimension of the horizontal universalism that has become the overarching normative principle. But we can remark that in "premodern" periods, in which social life was not already underpinned by such universalistic concern for equality of status, demands for equality still flourished. Individuals and groups might well have accepted partial forms of differentiated treatment, and yet they often insisted on being treated justly, that is, in term of receiving and giving whatever the symbolic framework at the time deemed "just." To preempt the example used in the discussion below, what the German peasants rejected in the war of 1525 was not the tithe or feudal justice, but the arbitrariness with which these were administered.[53] In their famous "twelve articles," they were at pains to present themselves as good Christians who understood the necessity for the tithe and feudal justice, and yet they were infuriated by the breach of the agreed code on the part of their rulers. They rebelled against serfdom, and the recrimination against arbitrariness and oppressive taxes can indeed be interpreted as a primitive demand for personal freedom. But these calls were made in the name of justice. Their calls for *Freiheit* were underpinned by a universalistic principle, namely, the *equal* moral standing of each and every person, as creatures sharing the *same* ontological status under God. Freedom in their argument was therefore a consequence of the equal status of all good Christians, a consequence of ontological equality. We might say that the normative basis of their demand for *Freiheit* was a primitive demand for justice, as a just treatment that *anyone* should be able to receive. A similar analysis can be conducted regarding many social struggles of the past.[54] Because of his historicist filter, Honneth can only interpret equality as a modern achievement. But historical hermeneutics proves that the primitive sense of justice of even the most oppressed has from time immemorial arisen when individuals have felt that they have not receive their due, or have had to give more than was right (in particular their bodily existence through work efforts, or indeed their life itself).

## RADICAL EQUALITY

Rancière makes equality the central principle in his own version of critical theory: "Equality is the only universal in politics."[55] From Honneth's point of view, the only way to describe such a principle, because of the function it has in Rancière's theory, is that it is a norm. Rancière, true to the "poststructuralist" suspicion toward normativity, wholly rejects this terminology. So how can equality be used as a principle to guide the critique of "postdemocratic" society or of hierarchically organized theories or as a principle to distinguish police from politics without being used in a "normative" way? Strictly speaking, Rancière would probably have to agree that used in the critical diagnosis of postdemocracy or as a critical guideline in responding to the philosophers who presume the existence of "the poor," equality is used in normative ways, as criterion for critique. But the highly specific way in which Rancière conceptualizes equality justifies his rejection of the term "norm" to designate it.

Equality, for Rancière, is a structural fact of society, a basic building block of any human communal life. Any "*arkhe*," that is, any principle (such as age, wealth, or knowledge) behind the hierarchies, which, from time immemorial, have structured societies, is fundamentally contingent, justified by nothing but its own self-given authority and the sheer power attached to it. Underneath the irreducible inequality that organizes all social life, there lurks therefore the ontological equality of anyone with anyone, an equality that is glimpsed at the rare moments of revolt when the contingency of domination becomes visible. At those moments, it becomes clear that anyone could in fact be in the position of anyone else. Equality, for Rancière, is therefore not a norm because it is a structural element of social life. This is what lends it its force, a force that is derived not from moral authority, but from the universal feature of being human and living in a human community: no order of domination, no hierarchical system can ever fully repress this fact of social life.

Equality, in Rancière, of course does have clear social, political, economic, and legal dimensions. In some passages, it almost sounds like the moral equality articulated by Kant, the equality due to every rational being qua rational, an equality of status.[56] Rancière's social equality can even mean something like an ethical equality, in the Hegelian sense of the term.[57] It is also an equality of capacities, when Rancière famously endorses Jacotot's idea of "equality of intelligence." But all those dimensions are only secondary manifestations of a more primordial sense, which is the "ontological," formal sense of the term.

Equality, for Rancière, is first of all a structural fact and secondly a method. The "method of equality" arises as a countermethod to the methods used in many areas of (European) political philosophy and the social sciences, in which a key aim of the theoretical exercise seems to be "the verification of inequality." This designates the circular enterprise consisting in highlighting through conceptual argument and empirical measures how social agents verify for themselves and in themselves, as it were, the multifarious social inequalities already postulated by theory. The method of equality reacts to this by verifying the effects of the opposite presupposition: in theory, it looks at what happens to political philosophy, to conceptions of the social, when the equality of the individuals (for instance, the equality of their capacity for reasoned discourse or for understanding) is posited, rather than their opposite. And in practice, it looks at what happens when people assumed to be incapable of acting or thinking for themselves actually act in such a way as to disprove this.

Rancière's emphasis on equality does not mean that he reverses Honneth's hierarchy of principles and grounds the value of freedom in equality. Rather, freedom, in Rancière, is one way to express the value of equality as antithetical, radically universalistic opposition to differential, hierarchical treatment. Freedom is the quality shared by each and every person inasmuch as they are considered from the perspective of equality, both in theory and in practice, both in themselves and for themselves. As a quality shared by all and thus as one that differentiates no one, it grounds no possible judgment of value, it is a nonquality. And it is a capacity that does not have to be attached to any substantial psychological reality.

Freedom and equality, in Rancière, are thus empty concepts. This is clearly another area where the Althusserian legacy has left its mark. His radical anti-subjectivism leads to a purely formal definition of equality and freedom. Equality is what allows different human beings to be compared when every natural difference has been bracketed. What remains is the pure, empty capacity to speak. Indeed, since speech cannot be relevant as the expression of anything natural or subjective, or indeed anything cultural or social, it is the capacity to speak rationally, to "think," that matters. Politics, for Rancière, is raising a claim in this capacity on the basis of a particular social site or type of experience in which that capacity is denied. But the claim is not about the specifics of that social site. Rather, it is about drawing the consequences that issue once people in that specific position are recognized as having the same empty universal validity as any other.

This formal approach to equality is very close to the one developed by another one of Althusser's philosophical successors in France, namely, Alain Badiou. Since we have witnessed the rise in recent years of an ontological approach within the broad field of critical theory, particularly in relation to political questions, for the purposes of the panorama this presentation seeks to sketch, it is worth dwelling briefly on some of the similarities and differences between Badiou's and Rancière's "critical theories."

Points of overlap between them are multiple. They share the rejection of cultural, psychological, anthropological, and phenomenological groundings of political claims; as a result, they share the rejection of identity as a relevant category for politics, which puts them at odds with many other currents in poststructuralist thought.[58] They both propound a conception of political agency based on the notion of a "subject without subjectivity." The political subject, for them, is limited to the intellectual and practical responses made by individuals, independent of the contentful aspects of their otherwise existing identities, to the objective demands arising from a radical rupture in the order of things, in other words, the demands arising from an "event." Only radical politics, politics that radically questions the order of things, merits the name of politics. Any other type of collective deliberation, expression, or self-organization only concerns the organization and reproduction of society in its "parts," that is, the hierarchically based apportioning of particular beings to specific functions via the specific mechanisms of "police" (Rancière) or "State" (Badiou) institutions. Any other form of social action, as Honneth would say, is for them in fact the negation of politics. It seems fair to say that their thoughts rely on an opposition that is typical of the post-Althusserian intellectual landscape in France, opposing political to social mechanisms.[59] Their dislike for psychology extends to sociology and is shared by many of their peers of the same generation.

A number of problems arise from such exclusivist conceptions of politics and such undifferentiated approaches to social reality. I will highlight only two problems that are shared by them to some extent, but in the end distinguish Rancière's from Badiou's conception.

To begin with, the relationship between equality and political practice is not entirely clear in their models. Since they both define politics as a radical rupture with the institutional logics that apportion social agents to particular functions, equality cannot be the aim of political action, since that would dissolve politics into social mechanisms. As Badiou writes, equality is "not an objective of action."[60] However, to refuse to make equality "an objective of action" seems problematic for a model of egalitarian politics, especially one that defines itself as being radical, that is, presumably, as intending to produce radical effects in reality. Indeed, in other passages, Badiou clearly has in view precisely those effects when he also defines politics as "producing the same" and "working to produce equality."[61] In this latter case, however, it is hard to see what differentiates in essence, or "ontologically," the "bad" state of the situation with which the event has produced a rupture and the new state of the situation as the outcome of the production of equality. For, if anything has to be "produced" in the serious sense of the term, if there has to be some truly productive "work" leading to equality, then surely that involves the collective coming together and organizing itself anew, in a mode that would still have to be called a "state of the situation," in the sense in which Badiou defines it,[62] even if that state is intrinsically different in its modalities from the previous one. After all, the ontological "state of the situation" and the political State are related only metaphorically,[63] so that it is conceivable that there would be an ontological state that would not be immediately captured in State institutions. Precisely, the new structures produced by the rupture with the existing order would be egalitarian ones, and achieving these would seem to be the point of egalitarian politics. The militancy of truth that defines political agency, that is, the faithfulness to an event that provoked a radical-egalitarian opening in the hierarchical structure of the state (of the situation), surely cannot be all there is to politics. That would reduce the content of politics to its mere subjective aspects; it would reduce politics to an aesthetic and rhetoric of rebellion without content. On the other hand, it is difficult to see how the objective dimension of politics could not involve precisely the kinds of collective expression, organization, and representation that Badiou so thoroughly rejects (indeed, his own movement is called Organisation politique). The universal that politics is intrinsically about cannot merely be the universal address retrospectively implied in a subjective embrace of an event; the universal involved in politics surely has to be also the "object" of politics.

Even though *Disagreement* seems to shares many assumptions with Badiou in a general sense, Rancière's model does not fall prey to exactly the same problem. As we saw above, in his definition of politics, Rancière puts the emphasis on the second-order issue of who is entitled to take part in collective deliberation over particular objects, spaces, and forms of experiences. The dissensus cannot directly concern the objects themselves, as this would dissolve politics into questions of "police order." But the objects, or the spaces, or the forms of experience over which a dissensus arises continue to be linked to the dissensus. Indeed, without them, there would be no dissensus. As a consequence of this, if a *litige* is truly resolved in favor of equality, the realization of equality in discourse (the recognition of the invisible beings as speaking beings) has to take effect through the realization of equality in relation to the objects or the structure of spaces that were at stake in the *litige*. "Those who have no part" would then receive their parts. Of course, this might immediately institute a new order of police and new forms of hierarchy and inequality. But the test of politics for Rancière does not just lie in the moment of rupture but also contains, at least as an indirect consequence, the social realization of equality. Indeed, if the proletarian studies of the 1970s are the source of his later ontological analyses, it can be noted that in these studies Rancière was particularly interested in concrete plans for organization. The positive model that inspired his critique of Althusser was the "association of free producers."[64]

Another issue concerns the relationship between theory and practice, philosophy and politics. Badiou consistently argues that philosophy is "under the condition" of politics as a specific "truth-procedure." This means that philosophy, whose specific epistemic fields and methods are ontological formalization and conceptual calculus, can only produce political arguments and conclusions by, as it were, learning from politics in the first place where and how it occurs. Philosophy, for Badiou, is appropriation in thought of the thought that is constitutive of real politics.[65] For philosophy to have any (philosophical) relevance, the thought involved in philosophy therefore has to be different from the thought involved in politics. The difference seems to be close to the difference between universal and particular: the thought involved in politics consists in the prescribing of, and following up on, the consequences of the axiom of equality at a particular site. If we take *Being and Event* as a guide, philosophy on the other hand seems to entail the thought of politics in general, the thinking of the essence or Idea of politics. Philosophy as a matter of fact can define the Idea of politics independently of real politics, that is, in pure formal, mathematical terms. So philosophy is under the condition of politics only in relation to particular political events, not in relation to the Idea of politics. Philosophy can define politics by itself, and in relation to real politics, its task is to "seize" in the form of the concept the thought that is developed there and then by political agents.[66]

The classical problem of the relationship between theory and practice, philosophy and politics, arises for the political ontology approach in particularly acute fashion. It can be noted that this is precisely the problem that, from the start, forced the Frankfurt School to engage in complex methodological reflections, and that explains many of its defining features, notably its insistent relationship to sociological and psychological scholarship.

Badiou in his philosophical texts on politics always refers substantially to the history of radical emancipatory movements (the French Revolution, the Paris Commune, or the Cultural Revolution in China), to the extent that his reconstructions of the onto-logy at play in those events look like a form of historical hermeneutics expressed in formal language, a translation of "real" radical politics in ontological categories analyzed in axiomatic style. Indeed, this would fit well with the idea that philosophy is under conditions of politics. But this cannot be the case, since philosophy is also able to define politics by itself in pure ontological terms. Indeed, this capacity is necessary if philosophy is to be able to produce philosophical "assessments" of political sequences, that is, judge political sequences armed with the ontological categories and expectations developed by philosophy.[67] We can see a circle emerge here regarding the relationship between the philosophical assessment of politics and political practice in the very foundations of philosophical discourse over politics. If the definition of politics as radical egalitarian rupture takes its referent from specific emancipatory experiences, then it cannot claim at the same time to arrive at a definition of politics in strictly immanent fashion, via a process of pure axiomatic deduction. The deduction is in fact only a formalization of real episodes. But if that's the case, then the highly specific conception of politics that separates true politics from false is justified in a circular fashion—in the end, it hangs only on a subjective decision without real justification: history provides the substance from which philosophy axiomatically deduces a definition of politics, but it is with the help of such formal categories that philosophy is able to extract the political substance from history. A different philosophical outlook, one concerned with other issues of justice, could just as well develop a different circular dance between historical instantiation and ontological deduction.

Rancière's mode of thinking and writing about politics seems to lead him into the same circle, namely, to project into political history the very categories that philosophy is supposed to learn from history. In the end, however, Rancière's more explicit hermeneutic dependence on historical movements seems to avoid this apparent circle. Rancière's "hermeneutic" approach means that, in principle, the evaluation of a real political action occurs from within, out of the immanent unfolding of the consequences of the discursive sequence that is studied and of the militant actions related to it. Indeed, since Rancière steadfastly refuses the language of normative categories, evaluations usually remain ambiguous. Rancière typically lets readers be the judge for themselves of where particular uses of discourse and types of action have led the agents. Or we might say that he lets history be the judge of how a political rupture would have evolved. Despite the superficial similarity of their "axiomatic" styles, Rancière's political ontology is in fact the explicit product of his critical historical hermeneutics; it explicitly formalizes the results of his long work in the archives of the "proletarian dream." Key passages of such historical hermeneutics provide direct resources for "ontological" arguments. If there is a process of formalization at play in Rancière, beyond the axiomatic rhetoric, it is a process of generalization from proletarian examples to all egalitarian politics. This is actually different from the practice consisting in formalizing paradigmatic examples, which are then reassessed formally, with history and ontology confirming each other in circular fashion.

## THE PROBLEM OF HISTORY

Both Rancière and Honneth take up methodological positions that can be described as historicist. For each of them, however, the historicist dimension of critical theory brings specific problems. Historicism is the methodological position which holds that key moral and political principles, or, as Honneth says, the normative fabric of a given epoch, change substantially over time, so that any relationship drawn between the past and the present, in either direction, is unwarranted. Critical analyses of the present do not apply in the past. And nothing can be deduced from past societies to our own. In particular, essentializing arguments that make normative points on the basis of features of the human that are supposed to be transhistorical are false. As the work of Foucault demonstrates, it takes an arduous work of historical reconstruction to grasp the specificity of an epoch, and that work shows precisely the extent to which the normative fabric of different epochs varies.

This seems to be one of the most commonly shared assumptions in the contemporary humanities in general, and in the different styles of "critical theory" in particular. For critical theorists, however, whose theoretical tasks are supposed to be defined in relation to collective struggles for emancipation, the skeptical consequence of historicism has a serious downfall. It prevents critical theory from establishing any link with "premodern" social movements, even if in some cases these might appear to bear striking similitude with modern ones. Indeed, it is often the case that critical theorists at one point or another in their writings forget the historicist imperative and relapse into continuist arguments between a past collective movement and modern politics. The problem is compounded for critical theorists who want to retain some sort of link, at whichever level that might be, with Marxism. For Marx and Engels were themselves strongly historicist, of course, always emphasizing the specificities of the modern mode of production and therefore also of contemporary politics. And yet, just as for Hegel, this historicism also accommodated a strong continuist line, made possible in particular by a tendency to reconstruct human history in a teleological way. As a result of this, past struggles for emancipation were often viewed by classical Marxists as direct anticipations of the revolution to come, just as past forms of domination and exploitation, however distinct they might have been, were also commensurable to the extent that they entailed social domination based on and expressed in the domination of the owners of the means of production over the workers.[68] In a text such as the *Peasant War in Germany*, for instance, Engels returned to the peasant struggles of the early sixteenth century to develop a political analysis based on a substantive comparison between these ancient social wars and the unfolding and ultimate failure of the 1848 revolution in Germany. Today, Badiou pursues this line of argument, with his anti-Hegelian claim that "history does not exist,"[69] combined with the appeal to something like a transhistory of emancipatory struggles, incarnated in the pantheon of the heroes of equality: Spartacus, Thomas Muenzer, Robespierre, Jacquou le Croquant, Toussaint L'Ouverture, Lenin, and Mao, to name but a few of the revolutionary heroes.[70]

How does Rancière deal with the historicist conundrum? Many passages in his writings appear to give credence to the idea that Rancière's position on that point is comparable to that of Badiou since there is a direct line running from the paradigmatic example of the Plebeians retreating on the Aventine and the nineteenth-century workers on whose behalf Blanqui was speaking.[71] In other passages, Rancière seems to rely on the idea that past proletarian struggles function like "inscriptions of equality" that leave their mark and become references for the struggles that follow.[72] These inscriptions are important in several ways. They provide not just historical examples in the exemplary sense of the term. They can also provide the discursive principles or tools that a political struggle requires to argue the case of equality.[73] And in many passages, Rancière argues along lines that directly echo Marx and Engels's famous pronouncement about the transhistorical presence of class domination beyond the diversity of its social forms, that is, the fact that all society obeys "laws of gravity," as Jacotot metaphorically said.[74] Both the police and the interruption of the police by egalitarian interventions appear to be universal features of human societies, at least those in which the rich and the poor, the free and the unfree, are divided. Honneth picks up on this when he repeatedly asks Rancière about the anthropological basis of his claims. For Honneth, this is the most obvious way to understand a categorization of politics that spans the centuries in such a direct and formal way.

On the other hand, Rancière is also explicit in his continued reliance on Althusser in rejecting the idea of history as a continuum, most especially if that continuum is supposed to be one of normative progress.[75] Furthermore, the historical material of choice, for Rancière, is obviously the nineteenth century. Rancière's historicism is most pronounced in his aesthetics, since the delineation of the regimes of the arts, at least in its initial presentation, ties the aesthetic regime substantially to modernity. To say this in a pointed way, *Aisthesis* might seek to replicate Auerbach's *Mimesis*, but while the latter spanned the whole history of realist literature from the New Testament to Virginia Woolf, Rancière's story starts with Winckelmann and German Romanticism. Rancière does make the point at times that the three regimes are not to be read as three stages in the unfolding of (Western) aesthetics. The ethical and the poetic regimes coexist in ancient Greece, and indeed the three regimes can be found in different modes of articulation in modern aesthetics. Cinema in particular combines the different regimes.[76] Nevertheless, the aesthetic regime is definitely specific to postrevolutionary society. Rancière might be antihistoricist in relation to politics, but he generally defends historicism in aesthetics. This might represent a problem for him since his politics and aesthetics are intrinsically related. Literarity, for instance, designates an essential aspect of politics, the availability of "the letter" (signifiers and signified) to everyone, which enables anyone to place themselves in a position to argue for equality, practically and discursively. But literarity is strongly associated with modernity.[77] It seems as though the suspicion inherited from Althusser toward transhistorical arguments is actually contradicted in several parts of his writings.

For Honneth, a similar problem arises. His position is unabashedly historicist, beyond the major shifts in his work. The three spheres of recognition as they are presented in *The Struggle for Recognition* arise from the historical emergence of new normative spheres, resulting from the demise of an obsolete way of grounding status in distinctions that are metaphysically shored up. Liberty, equality, fraternity, in Honneth's reconstruction, are new norms, without equivalent in the past. He reasserts this explicitly in his dialogue with Rancière.[78] In the new model presented in *Freedom's Right*, the spheres of recognition now take place in a more complex normative reconstruction, but modernity still represents a normative threshold below which critical theory need not go. Critical theory is the critical theory of modern society, and in order to conduct its critical work, it only need rely on modern norms, norms that allegedly appear for the first time with modern society. These assumptions are also the most commonly shared assumptions in contemporary social and political philosophy, to the extent that it would seem foolish to try to question them.[79]

In some of his earlier writings, however, Honneth felt the force of an appeal to past struggles. This comes out especially clearly in a text published just after *The Struggle for Recognition*, in which he sought to present Benjamin's philosophy of history as recognition of the emancipatory potential of past struggles.[80] Chapter 8 of *The Struggle for Recognition*, in which Honneth draws out the implications of his theory of recognition for the interpretation of social struggles, can be read in a manner that deemphasizes the restriction to "posttraditional society," so that the model becomes applicable and indeed allows one to make sense of, for example, the sixteenth-century peasant wars.

A significant problem related to historicism for an approach like that of Honneth concerns the normative teleology that is explicitly attached to his theory of modernity. Most if not all critical theory models today are historicist, simply because constructivism is the default position. But in most cases such historicism is combined with a critical stance toward the norms that are supposed to make up the specificity of modernity. Honneth, by contrast, has embraced a full-fledged teleological Hegelian narrative according to which a substantive completion of human freedom is achieved with modernity. This of course relates to the most basic bone of contention in the earlier confrontations between "French" and "German" critical theory models, namely, the normative appraisal of modernity. The model Honneth presents in *Freedom's Right* will encounter much criticism, from many corners of the critical field, because of this positive appraisal of the norms and principles of modernity. The criticism will most likely not be limited to Marxist critiques of neoliberal society. Honneth's analysis of modern society will also be at odds with the many authors who use the work of Foucault as their central inspiration. For these critical theorists, most particularly for Giorgio Agamben, arguably one of the most eminent and influential critical theorists today, the critical task in fact consists precisely in unveiling in Heideggerian fashion the potentials for oppression and violence that are hidden in modernity's defining categories and institutional principles.[81] Another important author to mention in this context, whose work presents theses and assumptions directly opposed to those of Honneth, is James Tully.[82] Tully has long been a critic of the methods of the Frankfurt School.[83] In recent years he has developed a rich model of "public philosophy," inspired by the Foucault of "What Is Enlightenment?," for a political philosophy that would be directly connected to real political practice, an alternative version therefore of the classical ideal of a unity of theory and practice devised by the Frankfurt School. In Tully's work, the Foucauldian reference is used not just to shore up the methodological features of his historicist and relativist agonistic position. Foucault is also used as a key inspiration for the powerful historical account Tully offers concerning the violence he claims was involved in the imposition of extraneous norms onto the bodies and minds of populations that were forcefully introduced to the institutional worlds of modern citizenship, as well as in the marginalization of populations reticent about these forms of governmental normalization. From the point of view of critical historical and conceptual narratives such as those developed recently by Agamben and Tully, Honneth's account of the rise of personal freedom in modernity will meet with the similar type of reaction Habermas encountered in the first wave of German versus French theory encounters. Conversely, of course, Honneth can ask of these authors the same type of questions that Habermas and the Habermasians asked of the French poststructuralists a few decades ago, namely, on what normative grounds, and through which articulation of normative criteria and factual knowledge, they base their dismissals of modernity and of its critical defenders. From the Honnethian perspective, it is simply inconsistent to denounce all reference to normativity while propounding a critical theory of society, since only a form of critique that is able to justify its criteria is theoretically sound. On this particular point, given the continued prevalence of the Foucauldian reference in the broad field of critical theory, the lines have not moved much between "normativists" and "anti-normativists" since the first skirmishes with Habermas. This most recent encounter between two eminent representatives of the German and French traditions of critical theory appears to be just a new episode in this well-entrenched debate.

# PART II

# A Critical Encounter

three

# CRITICAL QUESTIONS ON THE THEORY OF RECOGNITION

JACQUES RANCIÈRE

AT THE outset of our discussion, it might be important to recall a sentence that can be found in the foreword to *Disagreement*: if the invitation to debate is to bear any fruit, the encounter must identify its point of "disagreement."[1] Accordingly I will try to identify the kind of disagreement between *recognition* and *disagreement* that can make the discussion fruitful. The problem is further complicated by the fact that we are discussing concepts in translation. "Dis-agreement" renders the untranslatable term *mésentente*, which plays on the relation between *entendre*, to "hear," and *entendre*, to "understand." This relation between the two meanings of sense (sense as meaning and sense as perception) tends to be erased in the term "disagreement," which is less aesthetic and more juridical, and which presupposes relationships between already constituted persons regarding an object of disagreement. I suspect that the term "recognition" might also emphasize a relationship between already existing entities. So our joint intention to agree about our disagreement will be mediated by the relationship between three languages—German, French, and English. I think we must not deem it incidental. We have to take into account the distortion that is inherent in any process of communication. An act of communication is already an act of translation, located on a terrain that we don't master. This is also what is entailed in the notion of *mésentente*: the distortion at the heart of any mutual dialogue, at the heart of the form of universality on which dialogue relies.

It is important to raise this point in order to discard an issue that is often raised in the German-French philosophical discussion, namely, the issue of "relativism." On the German side, there is frequently the fear that if you take into account the distortion of the relationship along with the asymmetry of positions, you take on a "relativist" position and invalidate any claims of universal validity. For my part I believe the opposite might in fact be the case. Taking distortion and asymmetry into account leads to a more demanding form of universalism—a form of universalism that is not limited to the rule of the game but designates a permanent struggle to enlarge the restricted form of universalism that is the rule of the game, the invention of procedures that make the existing universal confront and supersede its limitations.

Now I come to the main point: how do recognition and the struggle for recognition fit with this idea of universality? As Axel Honneth puts it to work, the concept of recognition supposes a distancing from the usual meaning of the term. "Recognition" usually means two things. It means, first, the coincidence of an actual perception with a knowledge that we already possess, as when we recognize a place, a person, a situation, or an argument. Second, from a moral point of view, recognition means that we respond to the claim of other individuals who demand that we treat them as autonomous entities or equal persons. Both meanings are predicated on the idea of a substantive identity. In this sense, what is crucial is the "re-" of recognition. Recognition is an act of confirmation. By contrast, the philosophical concept of recognition focuses on the conditions behind such a confirmation; it focuses on the configuration of the field in which things, persons, situations, and arguments can be identified. It is not the confirmation of something already existing but the construction of the common world in which existences appear and are validated. In this case, recognition comes first. It is what allows us to know, to locate and identify anything in the first place. In the usual sense, recognition therefore means: I identify this voice, I understand what it tells me, I agree with his or her statement. But in its conceptual meaning, recognition is about something more fundamental: What exactly happens in my perceptual world and in my capacity to make sense with the sounds being issued by that mouth? How does it happen that I hear this voicing as an argument about something that we share, about a common world? When Aristotle distinguishes *logos* and *phonè*, this is a structure of recognition or, in my terms, a distribution of the sensible. This structure opens a field that is at once a field of identification and a field of conflict about identification, since it is always controversial whether the animal mouthing a voice in front of me is saying something common about the common. Speaking of recognition in terms of the struggle for recognition, as Axel Honneth does, clearly echoes this polemical idea of recognition. The point I would like to make here is this: How far does the concept that makes recognition the object of a struggle depart from the two presuppositions entailed in the usual meaning of the term, namely, the identification of preexisting entities and the idea of a response to a demand? How far does it depart from an identitarian conception of the subject and from the conception of social relations as mutual?

The question is worth asking because, at the heart of Axel Honneth's construction, there is a notion of the subject that has a strong consistency as a self-related identity, and there is also a strong emphasis on the community as a nexus of interrelations based on a model of mutual recognition. His theory of recognition is two things at once. It is a theory of the construction of the self, showing that the three requirements for this construction—self-confidence, self-respect, and self-esteem—are dependent on the mediation of an other. And it is a theory of the community asserting that the existence of a common world is a matter of intersubjective relationships: a community isn't a utilitarian gathering of individuals who need cooperation with other individuals for the fulfillment of their needs and legal regulation to be protected against their encroachments. It is made up of people who construct themselves to the extent that they construct, even through struggle, relations of confidence, respect, and esteem with other people. In that way an antisolipsist view of the individual chimes with an antiutilitarian view of the community. The tripartite division of love, rights, and solidarity is grounded in a similar principle. A common element can be found in a multiplicity of relationships: the child with his mother, the lover with the loved one, the juridical subject making contracts, the civil subject obeying the common law, or the political subject constructing a world of mutual recognition. The question is, do we need this common principle? Do we need to construct a theory of the subjective entity grounding the homology of all those relationships? And what is the cost of this homology? From my point of view, the cost might be the overstatement of identity, thinking the activity of a subject mainly as an affirmation of self-identity—even if, of course, it is quite different from many other discourses on identity.

Second, I think there may be an overstatement of the importance of the dual relation in the thinking of the community. For me, there is a risk here of losing sight of the operative aspects of the work of recognition. Axel Honneth openly starts from Hegel, that is, from a construction of the community around the notion of person: the person as an autonomous entity, able to identify itself as autonomous and knowing that the others identify him or her as such. At the same time, the person, of course, is able to answer for her acts, to account for them, to take on responsibility for them. I think the Hegelian schema is constructed around a juridical definition of the person. It seems to me that Axel Honneth's own contribution in this respect has two main aspects. First, he wants to enlarge this conception of personality by linking it to the givens of the anthropological construction of human individual identity. Second, he wants to supersede it by placing it in a dynamic construction of the community. My question is whether the latter, the dynamic construction of a community of equals, is not endangered by the former, the conception of personality as a kind of anthropological construct. This is why I think that the superseding may require a thinking of the subject that does without the anthropological-psychological model of the construction of the human self in general. It is not a question about the details of Axel Honneth's theory. It's a more general concern about the very idea of a general theory of the subject: for instance, the idea that if you want to develop a good model of politics, grounded in good normative presuppositions, you have to construct a general theory of the subject. I think there is a cost to pay for it, which is sometimes too expensive.

For instance, if we look at the place of love in the construction of the spheres and forms of recognition, Axel Honneth says at the beginning of the chapter "Patterns of Intersubjective Recognition: Love, Rights, and Solidarity" in *The Struggle for Recognition*: let us not get bogged down in the romantic idea of love as the sexual relation between two persons. As a response to this potential danger, he focuses on the relation of the baby to the mother, mostly through Winnicott. But can we really construct a general idea of love on the basis of the baby-mother relationship, which of course restricts it to the dialectic of dependency and independency, of symbiosis, separation, and mutual recognition? Can we attribute the traits of that relationship to love relationships in general? For the baby, his or her relationship to his or her mother is something given. Can we attribute the same traits to what we are used to calling love, which is, on the contrary, a matter of election, the construction of an object of love, the construction of a singular relationship among a multiplicity of possible relations?

Let us, for instance, suppose—and of course it's a foolish supposition—that instead of relying on Winnicott and the baby-mother relation, we rely on Proust. If we rely on Proust and the relation of the narrator to Albertine in *À la recherche du temps perdu*, love does not appear as the relation of one person to another. It is first and foremost the *construction* of this other. What appears at the beginning is the confused apparition of a multiplicity, an impersonal patch on a beach. Slowly the patch appears as a group of young girls, but is still a kind of impersonal patch. There are many metamorphoses in that patch, in the multiplicity of young girls, through to the moment when the narrator personifies this impersonal multiplicity, gives it the face of one person, the object of love, Albertine. He attempts to turn the multiplicity into an individual entity and to capture this entity, and to capture along with it the inaccessible world enclosed in her. He holds her captive, eventually she escapes. The escape of the prisoner is not the betrayal of a person by another person. The fact is that Albertine, the object of love, is a multiplicity of people, set up in a multiplicity of relationships and located in a multiplicity of places.

You might well say that this is pathological, that it is not love, or that it is bad love; and the novelist himself shows us that this love is a disease, a mistake. What the narrator was looking for, in the imagination of love, is what he will find in literature only. Writing alone will be able to do the right thing with the patch, while love is a bad choice or a disease. But what this work of art about the pathology of love tells us is that love entails a multiplicity of relations, most of which are asymmetric relations, and that it concerns the construction of a multiplicity of entities. Love is not exactly a relation between two people, but a relation between two multiplicities. And it is also a kind of construction, the construction of a landscape, of a universe that can include these multiplicities. So in a certain way it's a work of art. The loving subject is an artist, and I would say the subject in general has to be thought not simply as a self-related identity but as an artist. Subjectivity is a matter of operations, and those operations are alterations. There is a becoming-other in the very constitution of the other as an object of love.

Now this artistic, operative moment is also at work in the baby-mother relation as it is analyzed by Winnicott and by Axel Honneth after him. Let us think, for instance, of the role of the transitional object. Why is it a solution to the relation between the mother and the child? Because it opens a space of play, allowing the baby to work already as an artist, to construct himself, as he deals with objects that are both real and fictional. Even the baby is a builder of identity and alterity. Subjectivation in general entails this superseding of the "me and you" relationship. In a certain way, the creation of the space of play, as a space of alterations, supersedes the "me and you" relationship.

I focused on love first, but of course this tension between the subjective operations of alteration and the dual model is crucial in the conception of the political subject. We know that the struggle for recognition may be understood—and has often been understood—simply as the demand made by a subject already constituted to be recognized in his or her identity. For instance, there is a conception of the claims of minority groups as claims for the respect of their identity. But we can also conceive of them—and I think it is at the heart of the dialectics of recognition—as claims to *not be assigned* that identity. A minority claim is not only the claim to have one's culture and the like recognized; it's also a claim precisely to not be considered as a minority obeying special rules, having a special culture. It can be viewed as a claim to have the same rights and enjoy the same kind of respect or esteem as anybody, as all those who are not assigned any special identity.

I think this is important in the conception of the "struggle for recognition." Because if recognition is not merely a response to something already existing, if it is an original configuration of the common world, this means that individuals and groups are always, in some way, recognized with a place and a competence so that the struggle is not "for recognition," but for *another form* of recognition: a redistribution of the places, the identities, and the parts. Even the slaves were recognized a competence, but it was of course the other side of an incompetence. When it comes to slaves, and to the relation of slaves to language, Aristotle says that they understand language, of course, but they don't possess language. This shows that there is a form of recognition, they are recognized, they use language, they can use language in expert ways, and nevertheless they don't fully possess it. We also know, for instance, that during the French Revolution, there was a distinction between active and passive citizens. Only active citizens could vote and be elected. What was the principle of this distinction? An active citizen was not a citizen who did many things—usually they did nothing. An active citizen was a person who was able to speak for him- or herself, an independent person, which means an owner, somebody who doesn't depend on another person for his living. Of course, workers who had no personal property, who needed to ask masters for a job, were not independent people, they were not true persons. In a similar way, women were not true people, because they were dependent on their father or husband. Both were recognized, they were respected in a certain way. Workers could be praised for their technical ability and their courage at work; women could be and were in fact extolled as housewives, as mothers giving birth to babies, educating the future citizens, and so on. But this respect was precisely the flipside of a form of disrespect: both were coupled; since they were recognized in this specific respect, they were not in all other respects. So the respect of an identity may in fact signify a statement of incapacity.

To quote one last example, since it became topical again in France recently: in the French colonial system, the natives of the colony were French, but they were French "subjects," not French "citizens." In Muslim countries in particular, the argument was as follows: they are Muslims, and in Islam, there is no distinction between civil law and the religious law so we cannot impose a form of personality that contradicts the way they construct their individuality and their social relations. As we know, this colonial argument has often been taken up in recent times as a valid multicultural argument. This shows all the ambiguity of recognition. All those in my generation who were involved in political activism know how much workers could be extolled as fighters and as militants. As people trying to have their own say, however, it was a very different thing.

I am fully aware that in response to this problem the concept of the struggle for recognition proposes a dynamic model of the construction of identities. It's not a mere question of having one's identity recognized. As Axel Honneth states, the struggle itself creates new capabilities, and these capabilities need to be recognized. So there is a process of progressive integration. In a way, what is important is not identity but the enrichment or enlargement of identity: adding new capabilities, new competences. Those new qualities or capabilities are not recognized and this initiates a new struggle; it is inherently a principle of movement. The question that arises here is, what exactly is the telos of this movement? Axel Honneth says that we need some kind of faith in progress. Since the idea of progress is not so popular in our times, this is a courageous and militant assertion: "we need some kind of progress." We need it because the dynamic of struggle is a dynamic of enrichment, a dynamic of progressive integration of new capabilities. So the process has to be guided by a telos, which is a telos of integrity. I think, however, that, if the dynamic of enrichment is clear, it is not so clear what this "integrity" entails.

At this point, the question is: is it not the case that this process requires a concept of the subject that questions the identity model more radically, a concept of subject calling into question the wrong done by all forms of inclusion in terms of identity? This is why, instead of a progress toward an enriched form of integrity, I propose the model of the subject as self-constructed in a process of "subjectivization," and think of subjectivization first as "dis-identification." What disidentification means is first of all a certain kind of enunciation. In a political declaration, in political action, when a collective subject says, "We, the workers, are (or want, or say, and so on)," none of the terms defines an identity. The "we" is not the expression of an identity; it is an act of enunciation which creates the subject that it names. In particular, "workers" does not designate an already existing collective identity. It is an operator performing an opening. The real workers who construct this subject do it by breaking away from their given identity in the existing system of positions. This entails from my point of view a twofold excess with regard to this identity. First, it's a matter of affirming an equal capacity to discuss common affairs. It's a matter not only of claiming this capacity but of asserting it by enacting it. Those who make those statements do not protest against the denial of capacity; they enact the denied capacity. Again, they act as artists who make exist in a new configuration what doesn't exist in the present configuration. The key point is that they do not enact it as their capacity as a group, as the capacity possessed by the group of "the workers," but as the capacity possessed by those to which the capacity is denied in general. So they affirm the *common* capacity, the *universal* capacity as the capacity of those to whom it is denied in general, or the capacity of *anybody*. My point is that the dynamic comes from the enactment of this capacity which is beyond all specific capacities, that is, beyond any capacity that is recognized as being specific to particular social places, positions, or identity. It is the capacity of anyone or the capacity of the whoever as such. The society of inequality itself could not work without that capacity. Inequality has to presuppose equality. At the same time, it has to deny it. Political subjectivization enacts this capacity, which is denied by all distributions of social competences and identities. It constructs the stage of its own enacting. It's an asymmetrical construction because it constructs a world that at the same time exists and doesn't exist. So it is a way of locating the presence of equality within inequality in order to handle in the opposite way the relation of equality and inequality. Or, going back to the beginning, it's a polemical configuration of the universal. The issue is not relativism versus universalism, or universalism versus particularism. The fact is that in human relations, heretofore, universalism has always been particularized. So what is at work in political subjectivization is a polemical singularization of the difference of the universal in relation to itself. It's a way of breaking the closure of the universal, of reopening it. I think that it is probably the same problem Axel Honneth and I are trying to solve: how do we deal with asymmetry, or how do we deal with the nexus of equality and inequality? The difference between us lies in the way I make *equality* and not integrity the crucial concept and the motor of the political and subjective dynamic. If you choose some kind of integrity as your central concept, you have to presuppose some kind of historical telos. In a way, you can say that this solution is better, that it's more satisfactory since it allows you to use the idea of a global process and a global process is better than these "ups and downs" of political subjectivization. I've often been reproached for the fact that politics for me is only insurrection, so that, when no insurrection is taking place, there is no politics, everything is lost, and so on. But I think we can easily escape this presentation of the dilemma: it's not a question of uprising—or spontaneity—on the one side, and slow process on the other. The question is: how do we identify the motor behind the process of spreading the power of equality? Axel Honneth doesn't really like to use the word "equality." This is because he wants to construct a certain idea of the subject, and a certain idea of the relation between subjects, and a certain idea of the movement that allows this subject and this kind of relation to tend toward a full achievement, an achieved fulfillment. My problem with this is that in this case we have to presuppose some kind of telos, an orientation toward the future, some kind of motor of history. From my point of view, there is no motor of history: history does nothing. I know that, in a way, it is not very satisfying; but I think that it is the only way in which we can think equality, not as a kind of dream in the future, but as the power that is already at work in all our relations.

That was my attempt to reconstruct a kind of "Rancièrian" conception of the theory of recognition. Certainly that construction is open to all forms of disagreement.

four

# REMARKS ON THE PHILOSOPHICAL APPROACH OF JACQUES RANCIÈRE

AXEL HONNETH

LET ME begin by summarizing what I take to be the political ideas that Jacques Rancière presented in his work. These appear to involve two basic (but radical) philosophical moves: the first involves a redefinition of the so-called political order of society, and the second a redefinition of what should be called politics. In the following, I briefly reconstruct these moves and then analyze some of their implications. I hope that points of disagreement but also some interesting points of overlap or common concern will emerge from this.

## THE POLITICAL ORDER OF SOCIETY

I begin with the first radical step, namely, the redefinition of the so-called political order. In Rancière's view, such a political order consists in a legitimate form of government, which, according to tradition, is based on forms of mutual understanding described in either Arendtian or Habermasian terms; but, as he wants to show, this specific mode of political agreement always rests on the exclusion of some groups or people from the agreed-upon normative principles—thus all political agreements, throughout history and in all their possible forms, fundamentally rest on or are based upon an exclusion, that is, an exclusion of all those for whom there is no normative principle articulating their specific mode of existence. In a further step, Rancière also wants to show that such a political order (consisting in apparently agreed-upon principles that legitimate who has the right to govern) is reproduced via a process through which the normative principles become entrenched in visible and sensible forms: it consists not only in fictitious agreements on principles, but also in the establishment of a sensual world within which we only perceive what is dictated by the dominant categories. It is worthwhile to mention here that we both share this interest in the mechanisms of making people socially invisible.[1] The two aforementioned reasons—the basic mechanism of exclusion and the entrenchment of this mechanism in the sensible—allow Rancière to redefine what is traditionally called the "political" as the "police": "police" is therefore the name for an accepted or fictitiously accepted political order that rests upon exclusion and consists in modes of governing the sensible/visible world. (It might come as a surprise that I agree, to a certain degree, with this kind of description; I would only alter or nuance certain points—and this may be decisive—but I will return to this difference.)



## THE MEANING OF POLITICS

The second aforementioned step is the redefinition of politics, since the "political" has now been emptied of content. Politics no longer refers to the traditionally conceived kind of mutual agreement or public agreement about certain legitimate principles;

it has to find a new definition. So the introduction of the word "police" as the correct notion for a political order allows Rancière to redefine the political.

In contrast to the approach of traditional political philosophy, Rancière wants to reserve the notion of "politics" for those moments when the "police order," that is, the dominating political order, is called into question by interventions from those unaccounted for within existing principles of legitimation. "Unaccounted for" here means that there is no accepted language or category for their specific mode of existence and especially no category or language for their specific mode of suffering. A great deal of his efforts to rearticulate political philosophy therefore consists in the redescription of this mode of the "political," of the interruption of the political or the police order, by demonstrating and articulating its foundation in an exclusion. As I understand it, there are four specific traits that characterize the "political" in this sense. I briefly identify these four traits, which are most important according to Rancière's view of the political, as follows:

First, the interruption of the established order by those who do not count is only possible in negative terms, namely, by *demonstrating an injustice*. This is so, as Rancière shows, because the official language of legitimation does not include the categories or the vocabulary or the notions that are capable of making the exclusion and thus the suffering known. Therefore, the mode of the *political* as an intervention into the existing order always consists in the articulation of an injustice—a negative act—in calling something into question that cannot acceptably be called "just." So the first trait of the political is negative since it is not capable of giving a positive account of what is claimed; it can only articulate forms of injustice that have to remain negative, because they lack any possibility of adequate conceptualization.

Second, the motivational force behind these political moments (the event of the interruption of the existing order), which are always possible, is a deep-rooted desire for *egalitarianism*. Obviously Rancière wants to say that human beings as such—presupposing a kind of anthropology operating in the background of the theory—are *constituted* by a wish or a desire to be equal to all others. It is not a wish to be included or a desire to be ungoverned or to be free, but an *egalitarian desire* that brings about the exceptional *moment of politics*. So the basic category in the political anthropology of Rancière is an egalitarian desire.

Third, Rancière describes the political moment of interruption as the situation in which anonymous human beings constitute themselves as subjects. Here Rancière works with a distinction between identification and subjectivization, which differs from the usual terminology of French political theory and which I find extremely helpful. It differs completely from the Althusserian notion of subjectivization, for example, because Rancière attributes nearly the opposite meaning to it. Whereas within a police order people are only "identified" according to certain normative categories that derive from legitimating principles, it is only in moments of rebellion and interruption that they manage to "subjectivate" themselves. As Rancière would say, they deidentify themselves, which means they make themselves independent from the categorical identification within the given political order, and in so doing they articulate a new kind of subjectivity. In this sense, they make themselves political subjects by a negative intervention into the political order.

Fourth, what is for me the most interesting feature in Rancière's conception, the "political" is characterized by a specific type of speech act, which profoundly differs from the use of language we normally attribute to the process of political will-formation. Since there is no accepted language for those who are excluded, they cannot use the "we" pronoun, the first-person-plural pronoun, in order to articulate their interests or desires in the form of speech directed toward understanding.[2] Instead, they have to interrupt the logics of mutual understanding by making use of the third-person perspective in order to articulate the injustice of being excluded. At the same time their speech has to include a moment of aesthetic world-disclosure, because it aims at undermining the existing order of the sensual (or the existing fixation of the sensual). The "aesthetization" of politics is therefore not a specific trait of some contemporary tendencies in politics, but an internal component of all forms of "real" politics as modes of interruption.

I think Rancière's interpretation of the speech acts constituting politics is extremely interesting in two ways: If I understand correctly, this interpretation first and perhaps surprisingly indicates that the typical political intervention—in the sense of an interruption or "rupture"—is not articulated by using the first-person pronoun either in the singular or in the plural, because that would presuppose a shared language that would allow those who are excluded to already identify themselves and therefore would allow them to use the first-person perspective. Since that is not the case, they always have to refer to themselves via an indirect perspective, the perspective of a third person, which means they have to describe themselves from the third perspective. It also means that it is impossible to see that kind of speech act as being part of the ongoing process of mutual understanding, since it breaks out of it and doesn't conform to its logic. This speech act in fact uses a language that, according to the Habermasian description, doesn't allow it or doesn't allow it without further ado. Only the observer can take that perspective, but here Rancière is describing the participant simultaneously as observer and as participant, because he or she, or they, have to construct a description from an observer-perspective of their excluded capabilities and do so in negative terms.

The second interesting point for me relates to the world-disclosure component of this reading, for if there is no legitimate way of articulating one's own suffering, the political intervention has to consist in a mode of world-disclosure, which opens up a new sense of world, or at least shows the direction in which a new sense of world can be established. This is how I understand the core of Rancière's proposal, and I would now like to comment on it.

## QUESTIONS AND REMARKS

Leaving out any minor points of disagreement or doubt as well as all other points of agreement, I will limit my comments to three. I list these points of disagreement or points about which I am initially skeptical, not in order of their importance for the theory of Rancière, but in order of their logical sequence.

The first point concerns the presupposition of an egalitarian desire. The second concerns the description of a legitimate political order—the police, as Rancière calls it—which is based on the fictitious acceptance of normative justifying principles and also grounds political governments on the basis of social rankings, for example, age, virtue, degree of wealth, accomplishments, or whatever. In this case, I have a certain disagreement about the way in which he describes that legitimate political order as police. The third and final point concerns the definition of the mode of the political as the exercise or enactment of an interruption of the police order. Let me briefly expand on these in the following.

1. Concerning the presupposition of an egalitarian desire, it isn't clear to me how Rancière can justify the strong claim that the motivational force behind all interruptions of a police order is a deeply rooted desire for egalitarianism. Isn't the idea that we should treat one another as equals the result of a relatively late process of moral learning in human history? My suspicion would be that people in a number of earlier periods in history wouldn't have been able to make sense of such a demanding idea of equality. They probably wouldn't have been able to interpret their own claims as claims for equality, because they were living in a world that did not have *social equality* as part of its normative vocabulary. And if this were true (of the ancient Greek world or the Middle Ages), then it would be strange to presuppose an egalitarian desire. I would not even know exactly how to spell it out. Wouldn't it therefore be preferable or advisable to introduce the motivational force behind all such total interruptions in a more formal (and cautious) way? Candidates for such a deeply rooted need or desire—which my own theory of recognition as well as Rancière's theory both to a certain degree are in need of in order to be able to explain why there is this moment of rebellion against the existing political order—could be:

(a) The need to be included in a social order. This is what on a very formal level I would call the need for recognition, namely, the deep-rooted desire to be included in a social community as a member with a normative status.

(b) The wish or desire for a given order to be justified. Because we are reasonable beings, we need to have the order within which we are living legitimized. This would be a much more formally defined desire, which doesn't include as such any substantial normative component.

(c) The existential desire not to be governed by others, as we can see it articulated in some of the writings of Michel Foucault.

There are passages in Rancière's work in which he mentions a need for freedom, instead of an egalitarian desire. The last of the above candidates is perhaps of a similar nature: a need or a wish to not be governed by others is a deeply rooted desire to not be governed by any kind of institutionalized principle. I offer these three candidates, because I have difficulties locating Rancière's argument for the existence of such a deeply rooted, almost anthropologically given need for egalitarianism.

2. Concerning Rancière's description of the legitimate political order, allow me for a moment to identify what he describes as a police order with what I would call a recognitive order, that is, a stratified normative order of principles of recognition, which justify what we can legitimately claim as recognition. Indeed, I think he had in his remarks a certain tendency to do so. The use he makes of Aristotle would support this identification, for to say that a political order is characterized by the establishment of a normative principle that justifies an inequality between the subjects with reference to a certain social quality—and that principle can be either the principle of virtue, or of accomplishment, or, as in some earlier societies, of age—is to speak of principles of recognition. Such principles dictate how to recognize one another and, in that sense, they legitimate a certain political order. So the political order can be equated with a certain order of stratified principles of recognition, which then gets fixated—I would agree on this point—in the way we sensually perceive the world, which means that they determine the "sensible." If Rancière allows me this identification, then I suspect that his description of such a

political-social order is too rigid or too overregulated: all such principles, regardless of what they are, allow for new interpretations and appropriations, which lead to a higher degree of inclusion or a better way of understanding. So I think it is wrong to say that those principles—the principles that political orders use in order to legitimate themselves and especially to legitimate political government—are so fixed that conflicts about their meaning are not possible; I believe on the contrary that all such principles, whatever they are (even age, but especially virtue and accomplishment), are normative principles that themselves raise the question of how to understand them correctly. And therefore I think Rancière has to describe a political order not as a basically fixed order but as a social order or political government that in itself already entails the possibility of reinterpretation and reappropriation. I think this is extremely important when it comes to the question of the political.

3. If it were true that these principles are open for reappropriation and new interpretations, then it does not make sense to reserve the notion of the "political"—as a mode of intervention—only for those exceptional situations when the whole police order is called into question. We would need, rather, to draw a distinction between two types of such politics, which are both governed by specific modes of speech acts. I would like to conclude with a proposal for differentiating between two types of politics or political interventions.

The first type of political intervention concerns the generation of a new interpretation of one of the existing normative principles, which uses the language of the first-person plural and tries to convince the other side of the justifiability of a new appropriation or a new interpretation of the given principle. This is a form of politics that need not be understood as a form of interruption of the political order as such, but rather as a kind of *internal struggle for recognition*, as I would propose naming it, namely, a struggle for recognition that does not call into question the existing principles of recognition or the existing principles of normative legitimation, but calls into question the existing modes of their interpretation. These internal struggles for recognition are therefore not in need of a new type of speech act, as Rancière proposes, but can be enacted by using the existing modes of political communication, that is, by using the first-person-plural perspective, by trying to reidentify your own community with reference to a new interpretation of the already accepted normative principles. So this is a different kind of struggle than the one Rancière has in mind, but I don't see any reason not to call it a political intervention. I think we can differentiate from this kind of political intervention a second, more radical type: intervention as the enactment of an interruption.

The second type of political intervention concerns an interruption of the whole normative order, which doesn't aim at an improvement of the application of one principle, but at an overcoming of the authority of the order as such. I surmise that the political understood as this kind of interruption is relatively exceptional in history. It represents those moments in history when a specific social class, let's call it a collective of subjects, cannot find an acceptable notion for the description of their own modes of existence and suffering and therefore it has to call into question the entire apparatus of established normative principles. I think the typical example of this situation is the *bourgeois revolution*, wherein those belonging to that undefined class could only find a way for "subjectivization" by calling into question not just interpretations of specific normative principles, but the whole normative order. For there was no place within that order which allowed them to redress their own claims or kinds of sufferings. And in that sense, such an intervention is for me typically or traditionally called "revolution." I don't want to deny the possibility of revolution, but I think that the disadvantage of reserving the notion of the political only for those kinds of total interruption is that we are forced to ignore the daily experiences of revolt and political subversion, which do not aim at, and are not necessarily for, overcoming the political order as such, but which have a more (we would say traditionally) "reformist" ambition, that is, the ambition to simply reinterpret the existing normative principles. And I think the typical case of politics today is not the case of total interruption, but rather that of the internal struggle for recognition, which I would differentiate from what we might call the *external struggle for recognition*. With politics, or the "political," Rancière has in mind the external struggle for recognition. However, to deal with everyday politics in our kinds of society, where it is hard to see how to reformulate injustice in such a way that the whole political order is called into question, I think it's more important to deal with these small projects of redefinition or of reappropriation of the existing modes of political legitimation.

# five

# A CRITICAL DISCUSSION

THE FIRST *moment of the encounter between Axel Honneth and Jacques Rancière was the exchange of critical readings, through which each of the philosophers addressed questions to the other on his key work of political philosophy. The encounter then unfolded in a live discussion that took place in June 2009 in Frankfurt, inside the mythical building of the Institute for Social Research. This live encounter was moderated by Christoph Menke, whose line of questioning provided the framework for the debate reproduced in this section.*

*From Rancière's perspective, the key question revolved around the category of identity and the implications of using it as founding category for thinking politics. The reverse question that Axel Honneth asked Jacques Rancière concerned the idea of equality and how it could itself take up such a position. In each case, the two thinkers first had to react to the other's critical readings and the questions arising from them, and establish to what extent these were accurate representations of their thought. In each case, however, the critical questions also let interesting overlaps and proximities appear, leading to other, more constructive questions.*

*Throughout the exchange, it appears that the interpretations and presentations of the two thinkers' models stem from divergent perspectives relating to different models of critique as well as different understandings of what might be called the "political order of domination." Clearly a deep form of* mésentente *separates the models. As Christoph Menke suggested, this disagreement is also reflected at the level of method and style. Whereas Honneth uses what can be termed a "hermeneutic model," it might be said that an aesthetic model is at work on Rancière's side. Honneth's politics of recognition is "hermeneutic" in the sense that the political process for him consists in struggles around the interpretation and application of key normative principles. Rancière's model of politics is also based on a certain type of duality, but this time it is an aesthetic duality between the extant "sharing of the sensible" and activities that challenge that order and propose an alternative one. In both models, however, the political process is not centered on the claim of an emancipatory potential inscribed within reason itself. Rather, the very possibility of an exchange of reasons over particular aspects of the social order is at the heart of the political struggle for both thinkers. This might explain the overlaps that also appear during the discussion. The critical discussion between Honneth and Rancière unfolded on these key questions, as reproduced below. Christoph Menke invited Honneth to begin the discussion by responding to Rancière's concern that the critical potency of recognition theory was weakened by its reference to identity. Was there a place for the notion of dis-identification in his theory of recognition?*

**AXEL HONNETH:** I think there was a certain tendency in my thinking to describe the struggle for recognition in terms that assumed the positive affirmation of a certain identity—an already given identity. And I think this is not a completely correct description of what is going on in such a process, because it would presuppose something that we can't empirically presuppose, namely, that those who are fighting or struggling for recognition already have a full-fledged idea of their own personal or collective identity. In that sense, I would agree to a description of the—I wouldn't say the goal, because it has too much to do with intention—but the main result of a struggle for recognition, as being mostly a de-identification (or a dis-identification) in the following sense: that, by fighting and trying to reformulate the existing principles of recognition, we are losing the established categories of identification framing our own group, our own personality. In that sense we overcome our fixed identities. Let us take housewives as a typical case today: women who are struggling against their description as being housewives and nothing else, as being naturally inclined and disposed to do just the work that is conducted in the private realm of the house. To struggle for recognition does not mean to struggle for an already existing identity of a group. But I'm describing these struggles, like Rancière, mainly with the help of the notion of injustice: the experience of an injustice marks the beginning of the struggle, namely, the injustice entailed in a fixated description with reference to the existing normative principles. What happens in the struggle is the overcoming of that injustice, the reaction to that injustice, which then includes, I agree, a process of dis-identification.



## THE TELOS OF RECOGNITION

**HONNETH**: I would say that this issue is independent from the question of what the normative background of these struggles is. I continue to believe that in the normative background, what we can call the architectonic or the grammar of those struggles can be defined only in terms of self-relationships, which means of undistorted self-relationships. So the first experience of an injustice is the experience of a distorted self-relationship. I can't refer to myself sufficiently or completely with the help of the categories that exist in the political social order in which I live. In that sense, self-relationship is—normatively seen—the reference point of the struggles that I'm describing, and in that sense, something like the telos of an undistorted self-relationship is still what should be introduced here.

So Rancière is right in suggesting that I'm presupposing something: I'm presupposing a distinction between incomplete and complete self-relationships. But I agree that we are not able to describe what a complete undistorted self-relationship would ever be. In relation to this reference to an *undistorted* and *complete* self-relationship as the telos of the movement toward emancipation, my idea here is that even if we use the word "complete" as a kind of description of the telos, we are not forced to define what we mean with "complete." All we have are instances of distorted self-relationships. And distorted self-relationships are simply given when the social categories that are enacted in a political order do not allow the subject to perform a kind of self-identification. In my opinion, we simply cannot do without the notion of an undistorted and complete self-relationship, even if there is only ever going to be a negative or indirect access to it. We simply have to posit the ideal of an intact relation to self as counterfactual reference, against which distorted forms of self-relations appear as such. This ideal is what is meant by the norms of fulfillment, or self-realization, even if they are not the same. But in both cases we are also fully aware that we can't ever give a full factual description of what that would include. So it's a kind of "regulative" idea (this notion probably puts me in other difficulties), but as a kind of telos without which we can't describe the aims of these processes, movements, or political struggles, even though we know that we can never really establish the meaning of that complete self-relation once and for all.

A political struggle in that sense, as an internal struggle for recognition, normally starts with the experience of injustice indicated by an incomplete self-relationship, or (if we go into political psychology) by emotions of a specific kind. These emotions indicate the uneasiness with the existing categories of political recognition, which you then have to overcome. This overcoming can be described as a process of dis-identification and it leads to a reidentification. This process can be observed continuously. The telos of recognition—the ethical telos—would still be a kind of complete undistorted self-relationship. That is the way I would defend my proposal.



## THE STATUS OF EQUALITY

**JACQUES RANCIÈRE**: Concerning equality, I must say that I disagree with the idea that I make equality a kind of anthropological property. Honneth assumes that my position necessarily presupposes a "deep-rooted desire for egalitarianism." I don't think that I ever referred to such a desire. It's not a matter of desire. From my point of view, the fact is not that human beings desire in general, or desire equality. I don't know what human beings desire in general. I know that there are many ways in which what is possible for human beings and how they react to this framing of the possible can be structured. What they desire in general, I don't know.

Basically, my idea is not that there is politics because human beings desire equality. My idea is that the very definition of politics entails equality. In the definition of the political subject since

Aristotle, the political subject is the one who takes part in the fact of ruling and being ruled. This is something extraordinarily precise. Whereas there is a dissymmetry in all other relations, what is very important is that politics has to be thought as based on a symmetrical relationship. This is what makes the specificity of politics. Whenever the government is to be given to those who are superior because of their birth, their science, their age, or any other form of distinction, in short, whenever it is to be given to those who are entitled to rule because they have specific dispositions, there is no politics, which means there is no definition of a specific political identity. I wouldn't call it a norm: what comes first is not a norm, it's the idea of an entitlement, or the idea of a competence, quality, and so on. And it may be too much to call it an "idea." It imposes itself as sensory evidence preceding any judgment. So I think there are basically two logics: either those who rule are entitled to rule because they already exert a certain form of legitimate domination; or there is no entitlement. And there is politics in general when there is no such entitlement—in other words, when there is no dissymmetry. If the king governs because God entitled him to it, there is no problem, but there is no politics. . . . And of course, when the experts govern, there is also no problem, but there is no politics either. The basic idea of the political is this idea of a kind of shared competence that can't discriminate between those who are destined to rule, and those who are destined to be ruled. This is what I designated as the democratic principle: the absence of any criterion distinguishing those who are destined to rule from those who are destined to be ruled. If we read it in the reverse way, this means the presupposition of a competence of those who have no specific competence, a competence that is shared by everybody. This means for me that the democratic principle is not the principle of a specific government. It is the principle of politics itself. This principle comes as a supplement to all those that ground the exercise of the government in the capacity belonging to a specific category. There is politics to the extent that there is a political subject that implements the equal capacity of anybody. The existence of subjects like these is not necessary for a government to exist but it is necessary for politics to exist.

For me, the main point is the implication of equality in inequality itself. The point is not the normative distribution, and those who are outside; in a certain way the outside is inside. Politics has to be defined as the competence of those who have no specific competence. This is the basic ground, a kind of dialectics of politics, where disorder has to be included in order at a certain level. Our governments must legitimize themselves as the government of the people, the government of those who are not entitled to govern. They must declare equality as the principle of their action. But at the same time those who rule always try to get rid of that disorder. So there is the declaration that "it is a government of everybody," and yet at the same time, it is exerted by an oligarchy that legitimizes itself by its knowledge, its capacities, and so on. This means that political action is not necessarily the intervention of the outside: those who are not counted interrupting the whole system. To the extent that it is political, a social order has to include in some place, in some respect, this power of those who have no power, this power of those who are not included. I never said that politics only exists as an insurrection against the existing order. There are multiple forms of political subversion that don't imply a "global insurrection." And this is possible because the normative order has to include the contradiction in itself. For instance, the normative order of Republican France under the Revolution has to include the declaration of the rights of man. And the whole question then is: well, what about women? The declaration does not mention them as included. But it does not mention any exclusion. From this point on, the whole issue is about how you articulate the police principle of separate competences and the political principle of nondistinction. On the one hand, the police order locates them in the domestic sphere, which is a sphere of subordination. Consequently they cannot deal with the affairs of the community. On the other hand, there is this kind of declaration of equality that does not include any principle of exclusion; hence there is the possibility for women struggling for equality to say: "as women, we are men." In French, the word "man" has this equivocation, as both inclusion and partition. Women can say: as women, we can write a declaration of the rights of women. And they write this declaration, copied on the declaration of the rights of man. On the one hand, this is a form of subversion, but at the same time it's taken from the very letter of the text that is supposed to ground the normative order of the community. That would be my answer on the point of equality and on how equality is enacted in the political and in the action of politics. Precisely, the action involved in politics is a way of seizing the inner contradiction of the political order.

**HONNETH**: I understand the point, but I'm not sure whether it convinces me. The strategy is to say that all political orders as such, whatever they are, have as one or even probably as their constitutive component an egalitarian idea, namely, they have to describe what constitutes human beings.

**RANCIÈRE**: Not what constitutes human beings, but what constitutes those human beings as members of a political community. And of course it may be more or less related to an idea of man or human being in general. My main point is that to the extent that it is political, it has to rely on some principle of equality.

**HONNETH**: I think I would deny that one should call that equality. I agree that all kinds of political orders have to give a certain description or legitimation for who is included in the political community. Normally it works, as we said, through notions regarding who is excluded, so that they have to define those who are included in the political community. And the normal way of describing those included especially in the case that Rancière mentioned, namely, the case of the police, is to attribute to them certain human capacities like speaking or reasoning. I think I would deny that this would include any kind of reference to equality. For me, it is simply something like a definition of what is universally shared in that community, whereas the idea of equality would add something to that kind of original definition of the political community: namely, the idea that because we are sharing those attributes, like reasoning or speaking, we should have—only then can the conclusion come—the same kind of power to "political authorization," or something like that.

But if we don't make the second normative step, we can't speak of egalitarianism or equality as the constitutive trait of a political order. I can see why Rancière must stress this point, in order to avoid what I called an egalitarian desire. Because once you have established the point that all political communities are characterized by reference to equality, then you can say: everyone can draw upon this inbuilt reference to equality and can mobilize it in order to describe their own mode of existence as being unequal to those that are privileged according to this specific normative principle dictating the political order. So in your description, all government, all political orders have a certain tension between the reference to equality and the specific normative principle on which they base the legitimation or justification of their own form or government; this is an inbuilt tension.

We probably differ on this point because I don't see that there is this tension. There are other tensions and I would describe them differently, for example, with the help of the notion of inclusion and a social basis of exclusion. All kinds of political orders must refer to the idea of inclusion, so that there is an internal problem for them to justify forms of exclusion, and so on. But I don't exactly see that they must refer to the idea of equality in the normative sense, which Rancière has to make use of in order to overcome inequalities. That may be a point of difference between us.

## AESTHETIC MODEL VERSUS HERMENEUTIC MODEL

*After the exchange centered on each author's reactions to the interlocutor's critical readings and questions, the two philosophers discussed the methodological contrast highlighted by Christoph Menke, between hermeneutic and aesthetic models of politics.*

**HONNETH**: I'm not sure whether the distinction between hermeneutic and aesthetic models for the description of a political order of domination really convinces me. I agree that there are certain hermeneutic elements in my descriptions—elements that Jacques Rancière probably wouldn't include in his own description. But I don't see why it would prevent me from describing that political order which I approach in a hermeneutic way also in terms of a warranted sensible world, or as sensible world in which the order of domination has been entrenched. I find it extremely convincing to say that our way of perceiving the world is regulated by certain existing normative principles, so that our way of perceiving the world, of being able to see what "is the case" in the social order, is structured by the pregiven political categories and normative principles that allow the justification of inequalities and asymmetries. So perceiving is part of the fixation of the sensible; my gaze is part of what constitutes political order. In that sense, calling into question a specific interpretation of such normative principles also includes calling into question a way of perceiving things. This means, for example, that the housewife has to give a completely different description of what is perceivable in the social world of the household in order to make the claim she wants to make, namely, that the interpretation of an existing normative principle is misleading or wrong or incorrect. That includes always a new way of perceiving or of describing the sensible world. So I don't exactly see why there has to be a contradiction between these two models. The other way of formulating this is to say that I don't see why the aesthetic model of the normative principles or the political order, which I describe as an order of established normative principles that justify the asymmetries and exclusions in a society, why such an aesthetic model prevents us from seeing the interpretative possibilities underlying those principles. They are open for interpretation; they can be reappropriated. The aesthetic model does not exclude such redescription of the structure of those normative principles.

**RANCIÈRE**: In my view, there is no hermeneutics without an aesthetic, because aesthetics is about the construction of the stage and the construction of the position of the speakers. So it is about *who* is able to give an interpretation. The problem of interpretation concerns *who* is able to interpret, and *in what respect* he, or she, is able to interpret. In relation to the specific speech acts involved, the problem is not so much that the language does not exist for a particular social category and can't allow that category to identify itself. The problem is that the name of a subject names a position of speech that doesn't exist. So interpretation is made by people who are not allowed to interpret. For instance, in nineteenth-century France, when the universal suffrage is instituted for men and not for women, there is an important discussion about women's place, and many convincing arguments are put forward saying that if women are given the education of the sons, an education that must make them belong to the community of free equal men, then it is a contradiction to keep them out of that community. So many "scientific" justifications are given for an improvement of women's place. Indeed, there are even women who are scientists and who argue from a scientific point of view about women's civic capacity. Those arguments can even be borrowed from the normative principles at play in the police order. Many arguments in favor of feminism were borrowed from hygienist and eugenicist discourses. But it is one thing to interpret an existing principle as allowing for a possibility, or a capacity inherent in a category; it is quite another thing to allow a collective subject to "authorize" as such. Or simply to allow one woman to say: there are all those scientific arguments about the dignity of women, so I decide that I am a candidate for this election. The case arose in France in 1849:[1] one woman decided that she was going to be a candidate in the elections. She was not allowed to do so, but she still ran as a candidate. This was true subversion; precisely, the scientific arguments, however many, were not enough. The real question is about who is able to make the point and to say what those arguments bear, what conclusion can be drawn from those arguments. That's the main point for me: who interprets and in what respect we are located in the political community, as those who are concerned by the collective decisions or as those who take part in those decisions.

## IDENTITY, NORMS, AND SUBJECTIVITY

*These last considerations regarding the identity of the political subject forced the two thinkers to return to their initial point of divergence, namely, the form that the categories of subjectivity and identity should take in social criticism and in political theory. This part of the discussion also led them to reconsider one of the most fundamental issues at stake in their encounter, namely, the methodological question of the status of normativity, whether critical theory is forced to make its normative assumptions explicit or whether the language of normativity is to be avoided. Their diverging attitudes to normativity also informed their disagreement regarding the reference to suffering and social pathologies in the critical model.*

**RANCIÈRE**: I am far away from any conception in terms of the normal, normality, and pathology, because what disturbs me is the idea that the telos is some kind of good relation to oneself. I think it's a certain model of the subject, as defined by a good relation to oneself. For me, a subject is first of all a process of alteration. Similarly, social relations, interpersonal relations, are first of all operations of alteration. For me, it's quite dangerous to propound this idea of a kind of normativity defined in terms of the good relations to yourself: it generates an idea of struggle for recognition as a kind of reaction against a state of frustration. For me the point is not pathology and how to heal this pathology; the point is that we have conflicting ways of describing or constructing a common world. Of course, we can prefer one of those constructions to the other. But from my point of view, I would say that the construction in terms of completion of self-relation, of relation to oneself, is certainly not the way I would prefer to go about it. When Jeanne Deroin made this claim to be a candidate, she didn't need to run as a candidate in order to respond to a state of frustration or to a bad relation to herself. She did it in order to construct another world, another relation between the domestic and the political space. In the same way, Rosa Parks insisted that if she sat at that particular place in the bus, it was not because she was tired after a day at work. It was because it was her right and the right of all her sisters and brothers. For me, that's the point: what we have is not the normal and the pathological; in these cases we have a conflict of norms, or rather a conflict between two ways of framing a common world.

**HONNETH**: I'm not sure whether I would like to go on to the discussion on the exact status of the notion of pathology. The status of pathology in my thinking is very specific, and I'm not even sure it relates to the debate we're having here. I would not describe a person who is suffering from a certain infliction in his or her self-relationship as a person being in a pathological state. The idea for introducing modes of self-relationship as reference points for forms of injustice is to be able to give an explanation for different kinds of suffering under politically institutionalized forms of inequality or injustice. It means I have to explain why people are suffering. I think that Rancière also has to give an explanation for why people suffer from being excluded from a political order that intends—according to his description—to be an order of equality, but whose own established principles mean that it excludes a part or even the majority from the political community. One has to give an explanation for why there is suffering as a result of that state of affairs. We can't simply take it as a simple, phenomenologically describable situation. We have to build a bridge between subjectivity and the political order. And this, in my way of thinking, is made possible by introducing self-relationships as a reference point allowing me to build a bridge between forms of social and political order and forms of existing subjectivity. The core idea is to be able to give an explanation for the different forms of suffering. And they have to do with inflections of self-relationships. The notion of pathology, once again, is a more difficult case.

That allows me to come back to the redescription of love that Rancière made. I want to make it short. I found this description extremely illuminating. I'm not sure whether Rancière made one or two points. Let me describe what I take to be two separate points: The first point is about the poetic imagination that is included or is at the basis of all love relationships. You already said that. Even in taking Winnicott as a reference point, it is possible to see such imagination as a basic element of all kinds of love relationship, since the love of the child, of the infant, already starts with the fiction of a unity. In that sense, one could say that all love relationships start with the aesthetic fiction of a multiplicity of relationships, with a poetic fiction of some representable characteristics, with an aesthetic fiction. The fiction is about the loved one, the other; it is a fiction and part of that fiction is a fiction of unity. That's the first point.

The other point is that every love relationship is a relationship of relationships (I find this idea extremely interesting and I have to say that I was not sufficiently aware of that). In all loving relationships, we deal not only with one person but with a number of persons. You can also redescribe it psychoanalytically. But the point I want to make is the following: a pathological form—in my use of the word—of a loving relationship is when the poetic or the aesthetic fiction of the beginning is not "taken back" by the lover. If this poetic fiction remains, then there is a certain tendency to what I would call pathology of love. I think I'm in agreement here even with Proust, who would agree with that kind of description. If there is no frustration of that kind of fiction, then there is no recognition of the independence of the other, and in that sense there is not a "fulfilled" loving relationship. But that is another notion of pathology. I only wanted to agree with the fact that I'm using this vocabulary myself, I'm not nervous when somebody is using it, and I'm also using it with reference to all states of society, not only to individual states of affairs, even if, in the case I just reconstructed, I referred to an intersubjective relationship. In any case, my main point here is that in Rancière's theory as in mine, there has to be a reference to suffering. He himself uses the term of suffering. I myself would not have attributed it to his writing, but you can actually find it.

**RANCIÈRE**: Not so much . . .

**HONNETH**: Yes but still, you are using it. In introducing that word, "suffering," don't you have to establish a relation by yourself between the political order and the individual psyche in a very broad sense?

**RANCIÈRE**: Well, I resist precisely the attempt to think the relations of politics to subjectivity in those terms, because my point is that a political subject is not a suffering subject. A political subject is an invention; an invention has no self. The political subject has no self, so that you cannot account for the construction of the political subject out of the suffering of the individuals who are involved in the creation of this subject. In this sense, it is the same idea as in Proust's argument: you cannot account for the construction of a fiction from the needs, frustrations, and experiences of the individual. This is what I would call a process of subjectivization (and what is meant is a process of dis-identification). For me, there is no homology, no continuity from the suffering of the individuals in a given situation to the construction of a subject as such. This also means that it's not only a question of suffering;

it's the question of the construction of different universes, giving a different perceptual status and also different capacities to those who are included in this world. What's important for me is the affirmative aspect: we perform on a stage that was not made for our performance. The stage is not the stage on which we have to bring our suffering and try to hear it. That's why, as I said, it's very important for me not to have a general theory of the subject from which you could deduce what a subject in politics is.

**HONNETH:** I'm not completely satisfied with this idea. I see the danger of an overpsychologization of the political. And I also agree that political action in Rancière's terms—and I would partly take over those terms and that proposal—should probably be better described not with reference to the existing political order, but as a kind of interruption, or intervention into the political order and the existing social order. But given Rancière's way of describing an existing political order as police, he somehow has to build the notion of suffering into it, which means that he can't give a complete description of the political order without referring to the actual suffering of those not counted in it. In my view, Rancière owes us a tighter and more rigorous account of the relationships at stake here. It's not sufficient to say that there is a miscount, that some are not counted. One has to add that the miscounted also suffer from it; otherwise, it becomes unclear why they act as they do, why they perform "de-identification" and undergo the "subjectivization" process. Becoming a political subject means overcoming the status of an uncountable excluded subject; but as I like to put it, the motivational force for wanting to overcome this status has to stem from some form of suffering, which is therefore part of the political order Rancière and I are describing. It seems to me an added explanatory element is required at this place.

## SUFFERING AND POLITICS

**RANCIÈRE:** When I say that the political is grounded in equality, this means that equality itself is more than just a negative principle. There is no reason why some people should rule and others should be ruled. In a certain way, this defines the political subject in subtraction from all the relations that are relations of asymmetry. In that sense, equality appears as mere contingency, and politics appears as the form of community constructed on the contingency of domination and not on the justification of domination by some quality. But on the other hand, this kind of absence, of lack, can be filled, because it's possible to transform this absence of a specific capacity into a new capacity itself. The idea is that there is a potential included in the very notion of a capacity that is a capacity of anyone, the capacity to act as anyone, to act precisely in the name of the capacity, which is not the capacity of the teacher, of the doctor, and so on. The idea is a negative determination and at the same time opens a field of exploration into the potential within the capacity of anyone. What does it mean to act precisely in the name of a capacity that is a capacity of anyone, of those who have no specific capacity? In a way, you have the same kind of dialectic in art. In art, it is precisely a matter of doing something in person, reaching a capacity that is no longer your capacity as an artist. In politics, there is a possibility to explore the potentiality of what it means to act as equals. In this sense, it is a kind of open potentiality. But it has the benefits of not being normalized by certain ideas of the good self-relation. It's true that it defines some form of endlessness, so it means that we are not starting from mutilation or frustration to some kind of integrity, but we are starting from the mutual implication of inequality and equality and trying to handle it in a certain way, to make it bring about some effects. This is what I tried to say in distinguishing three terms: "the police," "politics," and "the political." I said that what we call the political—the fight for power, the action of the governments, lawmaking, the discussion about collective issues, and so on—consists in the tension between the police order that assigns groups and individuals to their place with their function and their capacity and the enactment of the egalitarian principle regarding the capacity of anybody. This means that political action is not simply the negative interruption of the police domination. It is a positive practice that concretely tips over the balance of equality and inequality. It inscribes effects of equality in our laws and our practices. And those inscriptions, in turn, allow new political conflicts and actions.

Another issue was raised by Stefan Gosepath in relation to this, namely, whether subjectivization is an individual or a collective process. He made the point that subjectivization is always thought by Honneth in dualistic terms, through the opposition between individual and society. What about subjectivization for me, and how do I think about the objective standards through which individual and society can be thought together, which Honneth articulates in terms of individual suffering and social pathology? In relation to this question whether it means that the people have to be thought as a whole, I would say that precisely you don't have, on the one side, the individual and, on the other side, the community, but politics is about the construction of collective subjects. At the same time, those collective subjects are not subjects defined by an identity. Instead, they are defined by the kind of reconfiguration of the given world that they can create. Again, I don't think that taking suffering as a starting point gives you a normative platform; it can only give you a normative platform in relation to a certain idea of normality. We all know that taking suffering as a starting point really doesn't mean that we start from anything that would be objectively given, since suffering precisely is also a kind of configuration of the situation. In the current situation, it is a tendency of the police order to interpret everything in terms of pathology: "there is a problem here, you have to heal it, to find the good solution." In cases where there is in fact a conflict of two worlds, they try to define a certain disease and find the good doctor. Precisely, in "something is wrong," the wrong cannot be defined in pathological terms. For me, it's the logic of police to define the wrong on a pathological basis. It's not necessarily because people are suffering that they act politically; acting politically, very often, comes because some forms of ruptures appear possible. I think it is a matter of reconfiguration of the field of the possible. It is very rare that suffering produces politics by itself. And we all know that the sociologists of suffering, for instance, present to us precisely a kind of world that cannot change. If you think of Bourdieu's *Weight of the World*,[2] in a certain way the suffering is always described as indefinitely self-reproducing. If we want to do something against "*la misère du monde*," precisely we have to remove it from this characterization as suffering. In other words, I think that we cannot break with the logic of the reproduction of suffering if we don't also break with the very language of suffering in approaching society and individuals.

Taking injustice as a starting point is not the same as starting from suffering. What is at the core of politics and emancipation is the invention of other ways of being, including even other ways of suffering. When I was working on the texts of workers in the movements of emancipation, it appeared clearly that in a certain way they had to invent a new kind of suffering. What mattered in those texts was not suffering from a lack of money, from the living conditions, and so on, but suffering from the denial of certain capacities; not suffering from hunger, but suffering from the fact of experiencing a broken time, things like that. . . . If we are thinking of this bridge between individual experience and collective subjectivization, I have in mind a letter of the joiner Gauny to one of his friends telling him he had to learn a new way of suffering. He recommends literature, because literature is the invention of another kind of suffering. He recommends to his fellow worker to read the romantic novels, Chateaubriand's *René* for instance, which means that the proletarian has to appropriate the kind of suffering that is the suffering of those sons of the bourgeoisie who do nothing, who have no place in society, precisely because they have a place in society. The point is the appropriating of the suffering of the other, and it is through the appropriation of the suffering of the other that there is an overcoming of the situation. If you suffer from hunger, low wages, and so on, it's not enough to get out of the situation of suffering. You also have to exchange your suffering against another, which at this point is precisely a kind of symbolic suffering, which concerns the symbolic partition of society between those who are counted as capable of this suffering and those who are not counted as capable of this suffering. The point is not being counted or not, but in what respect you are counted. It was very clear at the same time with the quarrels about the worker poets. Many workers were doing poetry, and all the bourgeois and also the great writers were saying to them: that's fine, but this is not proletarian poetry. You should make verses about work, songs for popular entertainment. What you do, instead, is write about high poetic feelings expressed in noble forms. But the point for those workers was precisely to take over those noble feelings that were not supposed to be theirs. This was also part of the process of de-identification at the basis of their political subjectivization.

**HONNETH**: I will only make two short remarks. I completely agree with what was just said, namely, that the reference to suffering can't present in any way a kind of normative argument. I agree with that: reference to suffering gives us nothing in the end to make normative claims. I think the reference to suffering is more necessary in my own view because of the need for explanations, not for normative justifications, that is, in order to explain why specific groups do dissent or do start to rebel. I think we can't do without a certain notion of suffering, which will allow us then to introduce emotions and political feelings in the framework of political explanation. I think that is a necessary step we have to do, because without that, you can't describe what is really going on. So that is the place of suffering in my own kind of conceptualization.

This brings me to a short remark about the question of subjectivization. I think it's necessary to think of subjectivization not only in terms of the individual but also in terms of community or groups. But in order to do that, we have to think of a group at least in a certain homology with the individual subject, which means we have to attribute to collective communities and groups the kinds of reactions and actions that we normally only reserve for the individual. That means we have to think of groups as first being able to make communal experiences when they suffer from the same kind of exclusion, and therefore aim at a collective subjectivization in your sense. I would defend the need for a certain kind of—I hesitate to say political psychology, because that is so inflected by the established disciplines we have under that name. But we are in need of something like that, let's call it political psychology, in order to be able to explain why certain groups do rebel under certain circumstances. I think you can probably avoid all that disciplinary investigation because I still suspect that your notion of the political is constructed from a completely external perspective. Even the fact that you tend to describe the political, the enactment of the political, as being a state of exception, which means . . .

**RANCIÈRE**: No. I don't think of it as a state of exception.

**HONNETH**: No? I thought so. The enactment of politics is the bracketing or the *epoche* of the existing normative order. In that sense, it is no longer internal, it probably gets its driving force from a reference to the promise of equality, which is inbuilt, according to your description, in all political communities. But politics only gets its driving force from it; the enactment of politics is itself a step outside of the normative order, and everything you are saying about that step and the way in which politics is enacted means that we are no longer like those political actors who are subjectivating themselves, as it were; we are no longer members of the existing society, we are acting outside of it. Therefore we have to be observers of ourselves; we have to bracket the existing normative order, and therefore I thought you would say that the situation is a situation of "exception"—"exception" is probably a word you should avoid anyway—but I thought you were going in that direction.

*The exchange between the two philosophers ends on this "disagreement" between them over the forms of critique and, in the end, over the forms of politics.*

# PART III

# The Method of Critical Theory: Propositions

*The book concludes with one text by Jacques Rancière and one by Axel Honneth. These texts make explicit the key methodological presuppositions of their models of critical theory and provide crucial material to better understand their positions in the contemporary scene. In the case of Honneth, one central question today concerns the impact of his shift to a Hegelian conception of freedom for his overall model. The text reproduced helps us to understand why Honneth felt he had to move from a quasi-transcendental or deep-psychological grounding of critical theory with Mead and the Jena Hegel to the new foundation relying on Hegel's mature theory of modern institutions. Similarly, Rancière's text clarifies the link between his well-known theses on politics and his continuing work on the philosophical and historical underpinnings of modern aesthetics.*

# THE METHOD OF EQUALITY

## Politics and Poetics

JACQUES RANCIÈRE

I GAVE this text the title: "The Method of Equality." I am aware there is something that sounds strange in the formula. Equality is not supposed to be a method. Equality is supposed to be either a fact—an effective relationship—or an ideal. And a method is supposed to be a set of procedures through which a definite effect can be produced or, at least, a path through which one must move to acquire a new knowledge or new practical abilities. On this basis, there are two usual ways of thinking about the relationship between method and equality. The first one consists in saying that a method is not committed to issues of equality and inequality. It is only committed to its own progress and results. The second one consists in saying that equality is certainly a good thing but that one must deal with it methodically. This means first defining what kind of equality you wish to achieve, secondly the path and steps by means of which it is possible to achieve it.

For instance, when I was young I was taught that political and social equality was certainly a nice purpose, but that for this to be reached, one had to proceed methodically. Domination and exploitation, so the argument went, are the effects of a whole mechanism of social relationships. Those who suffer from them are made passive because they ignore the laws governing that mechanism. They must be taught how inequality works in order to know how they can change it. Of course, it is not enough to know it. The point is acting according to that knowledge, shifting from passivity to activity. But at this point, it appeared that the most difficult thing was to know what to do on the basis of that science, in what circumstances it could be turned into action and how that could be done. I was warned that those who rebelled against the law of domination did it wrongly most of the time: some of them, because, as workers pinned down to their work place, they had no view of the global social structure; others, because, as petit-bourgeois intellectuals, they had no concrete experience of class exploitation, and so on and so forth.

* * *

At this point, the lesson of the science of inequality appeared to be a double-edged one: on the one hand, it taught that the dominated are dominated because they ignore the law of domination. But at the same time, it taught that this ignorance is the product of the very mechanism of domination. Domination was said to impose itself by appearing to its subjects in an inverted manner in the ideological mirror of their consciousness. So the method appeared to be a perfect circle. On the one hand, it said: people get pinned down to their place in the system of exploitation and oppression, because they don't know about the law of that exploitation or oppression. But on the other hand, it said: they don't know about it because the place where they are confined hinders them from seeing the structure that allots them that place. In short, the argument read as follows: They are where they are because they don't know why they are where they are. And they don't know why they are where they are because they are where they are. This theoretical circle resulted in an endless spiral: the possessors of social science were always one step ahead, always discovering a new form of subjection and inequality. They never stopped finding a new type of illusion in the forms of consciousness of those who thought they were acquiring science, a new form of inequality subjecting those who thought they were moving toward equality. They never stopped demonstrating that people were ignorant when they thought they knew something, passive when they thought they were active, subjected to exploitation by the very illusion of being free, and so on. The method for reaching equality in an indeterminate future was in fact a method for postponing it indefinitely. It was a method for endlessly reasserting the grip of inequality and the incapacity of those who were subjected to it to acquire by their own capacities the knowledge that could free them. It was a method for reproducing indefinitely the separation between those who know and those who ignore. It was, strictly speaking, a method of inequality, reasserting continuously the division between the learned ones and the ignorant ones.

That circle of domination and ignorance could thus be read as the modern and progressive version of an old narrative that was first formulated in its rough conservative version in Plato's *Republic*, namely, the identification of social hierarchy with a hierarchy of souls. Modern social science endlessly demonstrates why people stay at their place. But Plato had already dealt with the issue in a straightforward manner that made every future theory of ideology an academic joke. He said that there are two reasons why workers must stay at their place. The first reason is that they have no time to go elsewhere, because work does not wait, which appears to be merely an empirical fact. The second reason is that they have the aptitudes, the intellectual equipment that makes them fit for this occupation and for nothing else. So there is a perfect equation between an occupation and a mental equipment. According to that equation, being a worker is an occupation that entails that you have no time to be elsewhere than the place you are geared for occupying—which means that you have no time to chat on the agora, make decisions in the assembly, or look at shadows in theaters. This is what I call a distribution of the sensible: a relation between occupations and equipments, between being in a specific space and time, performing specific activities, and being endowed with capacities of seeing, saying, and doing that "fit" those activities. A distribution of the sensible is a set of relations between sense and sense, that is, between a form of sensory experience and an interpretation that makes sense of it. It is a matrix that defines a whole organization of the visible, the sayable, and the thinkable.

What exactly is the difference between the notion of the distribution of the sensible and the concept of ideology? The difference is as follows: the distribution of the sensible is not a matter of illusion or knowledge. It is a matter of consensus or dissensus. To understand what consensus means, let us go back to what is apparently a flaw in the Platonic demonstration. It is easy to understand that when you are in a place you cannot be elsewhere. What is trickier is to recognize that the individual who is in that place has the exact aptitude to be there and nowhere else. Plato, of course, had an answer for this: the latter, he says, is a myth. We have to accept a story or a lie: the story has it that God mixed iron in the makeup of the artisans while he mixed gold in the makeup of the legislators who are destined to deal with the common good. The story has to be believed. Now the key point is what "belief" means. Obviously Plato does not demand that the workers get the inner conviction that a deity truly mixed iron in their soul and gold in the soul of the rulers. It is enough that they *sense* it, that is, that they use their arms, their eyes, and their minds *as if* it were true. And they do even more so as this lie about "fitting" actually fits the reality of their condition. The ordering of social "occupations" works in the mode of this *as if*. Inequality works to the extent that one "believes" it, that one goes on using one's arms, eyes, and brains according to the distribution of the positions. This is what consensus means. And this is the way domination works.

From this point on, we can understand the signification of the science of inequality with which we were dealing at first. This science is a science of the verification of inequality, a verification of the verification that is performed by those who are subjected to it. The verification of the verification makes it more radical since it transforms the arbitrary story into a scientific demonstration. By the same token, it transforms the *as if* into an illusion. Plato said that the city should be organized as if the story of the division of the souls were true. Artisans did as if it were true by the very fact of doing their everyday job. But modern social science turned the practice of the *as if* into an illusion in their mind, an ideological delusion making them ignore the laws determining their condition. The method of inequality starts with the very distribution of the positions. There are two ways of doing so: Plato makes inequality a "story" that has to be believed in order to make inequality a reality. Modern social science makes inequality a reality and equality a goal to be reached from this starting point. But this simple dispositif is already the principle of an infinite reassertion of inequality. This is the point that was made as early as the 1820s by an extravagant French professor named Joseph Jacotot. At the time, all the progressive minds were concerned with the purpose of educating lower classes in order to make them move toward equality and take their part in modern society. Jacotot put the whole story upside down. He said that the method that pretends to move from inequality to equality is the way of perpetually reproducing inequality, since it continually makes the ignoramus lag behind the master. That is the bias of the pedagogical logic: the role of the schoolmaster is posited as the act of suppressing the distance between his knowledge and the ignorance of the ignorant. Unfortunately, in order to reduce the gap, he has to reinstate it ceaselessly. In order to replace ignorance with adequate knowledge, he must always run one step ahead of the ignorant and confirm the ignorance he is supposed to dismiss. By so doing, the presupposition that is at the core of the system is continually reproduced: the presupposition, namely, that there are two kinds of intelligence, or, in Platonic terms, two types of souls, iron souls that move in the darkness unless they are guided by golden souls who know the right path from darkness to light. Knowledge in fact means two things: it means the possession of this or that specific science, art, or practice, and it means the fact of occupying the position of one who knows. The master knows in two senses: because he knows grammar, arithmetic, or any other discipline, and because he occupies the position of the one who knows. And what the master knows is first and foremost the ignorance of the ignoramus. The same goes for the ignoramus: he knows what he has learned from the master and he knows that he would not know without the help of the master. In other words, his knowledge is a specific linkage of capacity and incapacity. If we translate the pedagogical logic in social terms, the artisan has the know-how of his job and he has—or he is supposed to have—the awareness that his lot in society is to perform his know-how for work that "does not wait" without caring for general issues about the organization of society. The progressive path from inequality to equality is entrapped in that logic, which is a logic of verification of inequality or what Jacotot calls a process of stultification that puts the subject that one is supposed to teach in the structural position of the ignoramus.

This means that there is no path from inequality to equality. There is either a path from equality to equality or a path from inequality to inequality. A method is always the verification of a presupposition and there are only two presuppositions: the presupposition of equality or the presupposition of inequality. What the presupposition of equality means is the rupture of the inegalitarian belief or inegalitarian knowledge. The name of this decision is emancipation. Emancipation is the decision to verify that there are not two kinds of souls or two kinds of intelligence. Intelligence is the same in all its operations and it belongs to everybody. All intelligences are equal, said Jacotot. This does not mean that all intellectual performances are equally valuable. This means that intelligence is the same in all its operations. The scientist constructing hypotheses and the young child listening and looking around proceed in the same basic way: they set out to discover what they don't know yet by tying it to what they already know. Theirs is not a path from ignorance to knowledge. It is a path from an existing knowledge to further knowledge. The method of inequality supposes that you must start from *this* point and try to reach *that* point by following one step after the other. The method of equality supposes that you can start from any point and that there are multiple paths that can be constructed to get to another point and still another one that is not predictable. There is a multiplicity of paths, a multiplicity of ways of constructing one's intellectual adventure, but a prior decision has to be made beforehand: the decision that one can do it because one participates in an intelligence that is the intelligence of anybody. Emancipation designates that prior decision to enact the capacity of anybody and verify it. There is no passage from ignorance to knowledge or from inequality to equality. Each situation can be dealt with either as an occasion for the verification of inequality or as an occasion for the verification of equality.

Jacotot had a pessimistic view about the possibilities of social change. He thought that only individuals could be emancipated so that they could live as equals in an unequal society. But this pessimistic view was turned upside down by the attempts of the workers who were his contemporaries to construct a world of equality within the world of inequality. Emancipation means that you must not wait to be taught about the mechanism of exploitation and domination. Such a mechanism is only too clear. What I called consensus means precisely the impossibility of ignoring it. Social emancipation began with the decision to ignore it. Ignoring it meant reconfiguring the way they occupied their space and time. Emancipation for those workers meant the attempt to get rid of the ways of being, seeing, saying, and doing that made them fit for their condition. What their texts first witness is the attempt to conquer the useless, the look of the aesthete, the language of the poet, or the time of the loiterer. It is the attempt to take the time that they "do not have" to go to the places where they are not supposed to have anything to do. There is no privileged starting point, said Jacotot. As a matter of fact, dissensus can start from an imperceptible modification of the forms of everyday experience. During the French Revolution of 1848, a revolutionary workers' newspaper publishes the long description by a joiner of the working day of the jobber who is laying the floor of a rich house. We could think that a workers' newspaper, in a time when revolutionary and counterrevolutionary forces are in open conflict, would have more urgent concerns. But precisely what is at work in this apparently plain description is a redescription, a reconfiguration of daily experience that invents a time and space of freedom and equality in the space and time where the jobber is exploited by a boss to build a house that he will never live in. To understand how it works, I quote a brief extract of his narration: "Believing himself at home, he loves the arrangement of a room, so long as he has not finished laying the floor. If the window opens out on a garden or commands a view of a picturesque horizon, he stops his arms and glides in imagination toward the spacious view to enjoy it better than the possessors of the neighbouring residences."[1]



* * *

Dissensus starts with a new belief: the joiner believes he is at home in the place where he is exploited. He enjoys the perspective through the window better than the possessors of the neighboring residences. In his *Critique of Judgement*, Kant made an apparently paradoxical statement about the disinterested character of the aesthetic judgement. He said that if I am asked whether I find this palace beautiful, I must let go of any "social" concern about the sweat of the workers that has been spent for serving the luxury of the rich and focus only on the form I am looking at. Aesthetic judgement is disinterested, which means that it does not look at its object as an object of knowledge or an object of desire. It is a power to appreciate appearance as such, and since this power has nothing to do with the reality of the object, it can be shared by anybody at all. That definition of the aesthetic judgement as "disinterested" judgement that can be shared by everybody has often been denounced as a typically idealistic view. A French sociologist, Pierre Bourdieu, devoted six hundred pages demonstrating that it denies social reality, which is that each class has the form of taste that befits its condition. But the core of emancipation is precisely the possibility of denying this kind of reality, the possibility of breaking the link between a social occupation and a mental equipment. The practice of dissensus actually started with the possibility of forgetting reality in favor of appearance and of casting a "disinterested" look on a building that is no longer an object of desire and frustration. The description made by the joiner gives that allegedly "idealistic" idea quite a materialistic meaning. The laborer stops his arms in order to let his eyes take possession of the place. His "disinterested" look means a disjunction between the activity of the hands and the activity of the eyes. We can call it an aesthetic experience. An aesthetic experience is not the experience of the aesthete enjoying art for art's sake. Quite the contrary, it is a redistribution of the sensible, a dissociation of the body of the Platonic artisan whose eyes were supposed to focus only on the work of his arms. It is a way of taking the time he does not have. This is what emancipation first means: an exercise of equality that is an experience of dissociation of the body, space, and time of work.

This exercise of equality has the apparently paradoxical effect of making the worker "less aware" of exploitation. The text of the joiner spells out very clearly this dialectic of emancipation: since no look of a master precipitates his movements, the jobber "believes" that his powers are his own. He does not even hesitate to call this belief a "delusion" and to tell the consequence of this delusion. As he puts it, "He believes he is obeying only the necessity of things, so much does his emancipation delude him. But the old society is there to treacherously sink its horrible scorpion claws into his being and ruin him before his time, deluding him about the excitement of the courage that he uses for the benefit of his enemy." He seems then to confess that the mastery he has gained is a mere illusion that contributes to his exploitation at the moment and to his unemployment later. But things are immediately overturned: this countereffect, which results from his way of reframing the space and the time of the exercise of his force of labor, is the source of a new pleasure, the pleasure of a new freedom in which even unemployment becomes a choice. I quote him: "This worker draws secret pleasure from the very uncertainty of his occupation." The surplus of physical force given for a short time to the powers of domination is exceeded by the surplus of freedom that has been gained for long in relation to the whole logic of domination. The same joiner invented for himself a countereconomy of everyday life, where all budget items—food, clothing, and the like—were calculated to both minimize expense and optimize freedom.

This is what dissensus means: dissociation between the know-how of a job and the awareness of a condition, between the exercise of the arms and the exercise of the eyes; it means the dismemberment of the worker's body, which was accustomed to domination, a revolution in the very balance of pain and pleasure. One thing, of course, must be emphasized, namely, the very fact of his writing the "narration" of this "day at work," the very fact of his getting into the world of writing. This is the point where aesthetics and politics mean the same thing. At the beginning of the *Politics*, Aristotle made the famous statement about man as a political animal. He said man is a political animal because he has the power of logos, the power of the speech that spells out issues of justice and injustice, while the other animals are restricted to the voice that expresses their feelings of pleasure and pain. I translated this statement by saying that man is a political animal because he is a literary animal. Now it is well known that the traditional distribution of the sensible has it that the major part of humankind is made of noisy animals, enclosed in the oral world of mere pain and pleasure. Therefore writing about this day at work did not mean expressing the pleasures and pains of the worker. It meant affirming himself as a literary animal. The power of the literary animal is the power of the sensible operation that is the preliminary condition of any justice: the possibility of exchanging a pain for another. This exchange is made possible by the appropriation of words, even in the form of a bad metaphor: the "scorpion claws" of exploitation. It is precisely this excess of the words that matters: exploitation has no scorpion claws. What matters is the very use of the metaphor, the very use of words that are not supposed to belong to the vocabulary of the everyday of the poor. Those words—the emancipated worker first found them in the random literature of the sheets of paper used by the grocers to wrap the vegetables, before getting to real books. In a letter to a friend, the same joiner tells him to "plunge into terrible readings" because, he says, "that will awaken passions in your wretched existence, and the laborer needs them to stand tall in the face of that which is ready to devour him." What is needed in the process of emancipation is first and foremost passions. As has been well known since Plato, passion means a certain balance of pleasure and pain. What is provided by writing and reading is a new way, a human way, of feeling pleasure and pain. This is why the "terrible readings" he recommends to his friends are not books describing the horrors of capitalism and the wretched condition of the poor. On the contrary, he recommends to him the books of the great romantic writers. Those books told the misfortunes of characters whose sorrow was that of not having a place and an occupation in society, of being born for no definite job or task, of having "nothing to do" out of their life. This was not the case of those workers, indeed: they suffered from the contrary, from the fact of having a place in society, of being born for a definite way of living and doing and being unable to escape that necessity. But this is what literature is about: exchanging one's pain for another's pain. And this is what those workers needed: exchanging their pain for another's pain; making their voice not the voice of their condition but the voice of anybody, the expression of the capacity of anybody, confronting the social distribution of capacities and incapacities. The same goes for those "terrible readings" as for the reframing of the time and space of labor operated by the joiner: those forms of "aesthetic experience" do not work by providing definite messages or conveying specific forms of energy. They work by disrupting the way in which bodies fit their functions and destinations.

That disruption started with what was the very condition for reading and writing, namely, using for them a time that was normally dedicated to sleep. The very core of the distribution of the sensible is the division of night and day. This division is the least escapable partition of time, the least escapable separation between those who can and cannot play with it. The division has it that those who work all day long must sleep during the night to restore their force and go back to work heartedly the following day. This is why the core of emancipation was the intellectual decision and the physical attempt to break this circle, to put off as long as possible the entry into sleep and use this time for reading, writing, and discussing, for composing workers' newspapers or poetry, if not both of them. The core of the process of emancipation could be located in that quasi-imperceptible interruption of the normal round of work and repose, allowing those workers to both prepare for the future and live in the present the suspension of the hierarchy subordinating those dedicated to manual labor to those dedicated to the task of thinking. Emancipated workers were workers who constructed for themselves in the here and now a new body and a new soul, the body or the soul of those fitted for no specific occupation, but who put into work the capacities of seeing and speaking, thinking and doing that belong to no class in particular, that belong to anybody. It is this affirmation that linked the apparently harmless practice of writing poetry to the creation of workers' newspapers and the capacity to build cooperatives of workers, republican barricades, and the organizations for class war. As emancipation entails a reconfiguration of the sensible world, it dismisses the classical oppositions between the means and the ends. The time of emancipation creates no opposition between the present and the future, in the same way as it creates no opposition between lived experience and strategic designs or between the discovery of private life and the construction of collective forms of life. This is why this apparently plain description of the day-at-work of a solitary joiner was at its right place in a worker's journal in a time of revolution. A workers' journal is not the expression of the workers' sufferings and demands. It is a break away from the old distribution of the sensible that divides humankind in two categories: those who can only shout to express their pains and complaints, and those who are able to discuss matters of justice concerning the whole community; those who are enclosed in the circle of so-called oral culture and those who live in the universe of writing. It is the affirmation of their capacity to reconstruct their world of experience, therefore to take their part in the global reconfiguration of the social world. A political capacity is the product of an aesthetic revolution. An aesthetic revolution is not a revolution in the arts. It is a revolution in the distribution of the forms and capacities of experience that this or that social group can share. Those forms of "aesthetic experience," those forms of appropriation of the power of words, do not work by providing definite messages or conveying specific forms of energy. They work by disrupting the way in which bodies fit their functions and destinations. They don't frame a collective body. Instead, they produce a multiplicity of folds and gaps in the fabric of common experience that change the cartography of the perceptible, the thinkable, and the feasible. As such, they allow for new modes of political construction of common objects and new possibilities of collective enunciation. The aesthetic effect is an effect of dis-identification. As such, it is political because political subjectivization proceeds via a process of dis-identification. The "voice of the workers" is the voice of workers who no longer feel and speak the way they did as dominated workers, when they were verifying the inequality that pinned them down to their place.

* * *

This is what I call a verification of equality, the implementation of a method of equality: a way of reconstructing a given form of everyday sensible experience so as to tip the balance of equality and inequality that is at work in every situation. Now I'd like to emphasize a key aspect of this method. In order to construct his new gaze, the joiner had to borrow the perspective and the gaze that were the privilege of the masters or of the artists. In order to voice his experience in a newspaper that is the voice of the workers, he had to exchange the everyday pain of those who are exploited at work for the immaterial pain of the literary characters who have "nothing to do" in society. He had to cross the boundaries separating forms of experience, modes of visibility, and also usages of language—such as the boundary separating the language of everyday experience and the language of literature or the boundaries separating literary fiction, social, knowledge and political statement. The method of equality goes across the boundaries of genres and levels of discourse. Now my point is that this condition for a verification of equality is also the condition for the discourse that sets out to make sense of that verification. It has to verify equality itself, that is to say, it has to refuse to set itself in a genre or level of discourse different from the discourse it is dealing with. It has to practice what I called a poetics of knowledge.

A poetics of knowledge does not mean that all knowledge is mere fiction. It has nothing to do with any kind of skepticism or relativism in relation to truth. On the contrary, it means that, to deal with the truth of a discourse, we must turn down the position of the scientist and reinscribe one's descriptions and arguments in the equality of common language and the common capacity of thinking, the common capacity to invent stories and arguments. This means that we have to undo the logic of inequality that is at work in the discourse of science, that is, in the discourse of the disciplines that purport to make sense of those narrations. For those disciplines, "making sense" of a discourse means "giving the meaning of it" or explaining it. By grabbing hold of the narrative of the joiner, the sociologist or the social historian undoes his egalitarian performance. They annul the dissociation between the gaze and the arms of the joiner. They replace it with another one, an inegalitarian one: they draw a line of separation between what the phrases of the joiner say and what they mean, between their raw materiality and the social situation that they express. By so doing, they deny this discourse the possession of its own sense. For instance, social history restages the egalitarian operation by which the joiner reframed the place and job involved in his work. It explains it as the expression of the ambiguous situation and contradictory consciousness of the artisans of his time. Cultural sociology, for its part, explains his way of borrowing the writing of the writers and the feelings of their characters as the mark of his being ensnared in the forms of dominant culture. It turns the "disinterested" look into a philosophical and petty-bourgeois illusion that can only cheat the poor artisan, and so on and so forth. Disciplinary discourses then reinstate the boundary between two ways of using language: a way of using it to express a situation, and a way of using it to explain what this situation is and why it expresses itself in this or that way. They reinstate the presupposition of inequality between two uses of language, two kinds of intelligence, and two classes of souls. They don't do so by any kind of malevolence. They do so because the presupposition of inequality is the condition of their exercise. They want, for the sake of their own validity, what Plato wanted for the sake of good social order: that the bodies composing society have the perceptions, sensations, and thoughts that correspond to their space and time, to their situation and their occupation. In order to establish themselves as scientific disciplines, they have to cut inside the fabric of common thought and common language to divide it in two parts: on one side, modes of thought and language that are the "object" of science; on the other one, modes of thought and language that are the forms of scientific description and argumentation. A discipline, in effect, is not merely the exploitation of a territory and the definition of a set of methods appropriate to a certain domain or a certain type of object. The very division between disciplines is first and foremost a way to say, you must not go there, unless you have the qualification for doing so. It inscribes the presupposition of competence or incompetence in the very landscape of the perceptible and the thinkable. The so-called division of labor between disciplines is in reality a war. It is a war for fixing boundaries, starting with the strategic boundary separating those who know from those who don't know.

A poetics of knowledge thus is a practice of "indisciplinary" thinking. It refuses the "disciplinary" logic, its alleged specialization in fields, objects, and methods and the presupposition of the separation between those who know and those who don't know. The poetics of knowledge starts from the presupposition of equality. The presupposition of equality does not claim that all discourses are equally valuable. It claims that there is a capacity for thinking that does not belong to any special group, a capacity that can be attributed to anybody. There is therefore a way of looking at all forms of discourse from the point of view of that capacity. This means that no positive boundary severs the field of sociology from the field of philosophy, or the field of history from the field of literature, and so on. All disciplines contend that they have their objects and the methods fitting them. The poetics of knowledge responds to this: your objects belong to everybody, your methods belong to anybody. They are made of narrations and descriptions that are told in a language that is the language of anybody and of arguments that are relevant to the intelligence of anybody. This also means that no positive boundary separates the texts that make up the discourse of science from those that are merely the objects of science. Ultimately no positive boundary separates those who are fit for thinking from those who are not fit for that. What we deal with are different performances of the "literary animal." To make sense of them, the point is not "explaining" them. It is weaving a fabric of language within which they can experience egalitarian connections with other performances situated in different historical contexts pertaining to different fields. This is what I decided to do, for my part: to weave a kind of poetic fabric of writing that was not identifiable either with philosophy or with history, with science or with literature. I was dealing with a material made of workers' pamphlets, poems, letters, and narratives as well. I decided to extract those texts from the context of social history, in which they were treated as expressions of a certain workers' culture. Those texts were dealing with matters of work, time and space, voice and speech, visibility and invisibility. They were dealing with issues of capacity and incapacity, of who is able or unable to decide about matters of work and community. So they were narrations, statements, and arguments about the distribution of the sensible and interventions in that distribution. As such, they could be connected with other narratives and other interventions, borrowed from literary or philosophical texts, in other times and other contexts. Plato wrote about the necessity for workers to stay at their place because work does not wait. He explained that those workers had to do it because they were born with the aptitudes fitting that life. Nineteenth-century workers, for their part, wrote about the possibility or impossibility of escaping the constraint of time and the kind of life for which workers were born. Plato and those workers did not live in the same time and the same kind of society, nor are they dealing with the same kind of work, for sure. Nevertheless it was possible to make the hypothesis that they were dealing with one common issue, namely, the relation between conditions and capacities, between being in a certain time and space and being endowed with certain capacities and incapacities. It was possible to verify it by stepping across the differences of times, genres, and levels. This is an exercise in the method of equality that draws the treatise of the philosopher, the verse of the poet, the narration of the historian, and the article of the worker out of their "specific" territory and status and considers them as performances of speaking beings about what it means to be a speaking being. The poetics of knowledge gets to the point where even the statement of inequality must be formulated in an egalitarian way. This is the case for the Platonic statement about the inequality of the souls. It must be told as a story. It is when we speak of truth, Plato claims in the *Phaedrus*, that we are most obliged to say the truth. It is at that point also that he has recourse to the most extravagant tale: he tells us that the hierarchy of conditions rests on a hierarchy of souls and that such hierarchy depends on their respective capacity to follow the divine charioteer and look at divine beauty while traveling in the plain of truth. Those who have seen more fall into the bodies of philosophers or kings, those who have seen less into the bodies of artisans, peasants, or sophists. In this way, the social hierarchy is tantamount to the hierarchy of knowledge. But this equation, which most implacably prescribes the distribution of conditions, identities, and competences, can be told precisely only in the genre of discourse that denies any hierarchy, the genre of discourse that is practiced by the most "ignorant" ones, the genre of the tale. When it comes to truth and more particularly to the relation of truth to social hierarchy, all hierarchies of genres and levels of discourse are abolished. The poetics of knowledge deals with this knot between equality and inequality, it deals with the way in which it is tied and untied to the advantage of equality or inequality. It does not purport to provide a better knowledge than the knowledge provided by the disciplines. Rather, it tries to question how this or that form of knowledge deals with the circulation of words by which human animals are pinned down to their place or get away from it. It does not purport to provide instructions or forms of energy for any specific struggle. Rather, it tries to foster forms of intellectual indiscipline, forms of sensitivity and intolerance toward the multiple ways in which the method of inequality is at work in arguments, stories, or images and most notably in those that purport to lead us on the path of equality.

This leads me back to my starting point: the way in which inequality was indefinitely reproduced in the process that was said to lead to a future of equality, that is, the way in which the idea and practice of emancipation have been historically blended with a quite different idea of domination and liberation and, in the end, subjected to it, the one that made emancipation the end point of a global process that could be handled only by those who knew the logic of social evolution and the way to put this knowledge at work. On this basis, emancipation was no longer conceived as the construction of new capacities. It was the promise of science to those whose illusory capacities could be nothing but the reverse side of their real incapacity. But the very logic of science was that of an endless deferment of the promise. The science that promised freedom was also the science of the total process whose effect is to endlessly generate its own ignorance. That is why it constantly had to set about deciphering deceptive images and unmasking the illusory forms of self-enrichment, which could only enclose individuals in the trap of illusion, subjection, and misery each time a bit more.

It might be said that this scenario of the promises of science is a scenario of another age, a scenario whose final death was recorded in 1989. We are said to live in a postmodern era in which the critique of domination and the narrative of the revolutionary promise have come to an end with all modernist scenarios and illusions. But what died in 1989 is the promise of emancipation linked with the endless critique of the illusions produced by the system of domination. It is the promise of equality linked with the method of eternally reproducing inequality, not the method itself. The method itself is still at work. Day after day, we are told about the ways in which the global system of domination grabs hold of us and cheats us. We are told about the illusions of freedom and equality that hide the reality of domination by global capitalism, about the progress of all the technologies of power and biopower that take control of our bodies and our minds, about the frenzy of consumption that enslaves us all to the law of the global market, about the empire of the spectacle that transforms any reality into illusion, and so on and so forth. All those themes were present in the culture of Western critical and progressive thought in the 1960s. At the time, they were supposed to provide those who challenged the system with weapons for their struggle. What happened in the meantime is that those themes have been severed from any horizon of emancipation. The demonstration of incapacity has been stripped of any promise of liberation through knowledge. On the contrary, it tends more and more to tell us why emancipation is impossible by depicting for us a world where the forces of domination are omnipotent, a world of narcissist individuals whose desires, even the desires of protest and rebellion, are entirely caught in the machine of domination, recuperated as instruments of subjection. The critique of domination ends up as a critique of liberation. In the end, the revolutionary denunciation of social mechanisms becomes the apocalyptic prophecy of the impending catastrophe. What remains the core of the method, through all its shifts and reversals, is the presupposition of inequality, the presupposition of the radical separation between a world doomed to ignorance and the very few who know about the way either toward a new society or toward an impending disaster.

I am certainly not willing to deny the force of all the machineries of domination today. Nor am I willing to propose any optimistic view of the future in reaction to that apocalyptic mood.

My point is that any attempt at resisting those forces starts with the rejection of the assumptions of the method of inequality: the assumptions of the global process, the idea of the mechanism of domination as a mechanism of illusion, in short, the presupposition of inequality. The apocalyptic mood is a consequence of the very faith in a global process revealing in the end a truth hidden to its subjects. That is why a method of equality does not propose a countermodel of the future. It does not construct a model showing how to go from the present to an already-known goal. Rather, it insists on the division that is at work at every point of every process. There is no global process creating its own machinery and absorbing all rebellious energies. Rather, there is a multiplicity of forms and scenes of dissensus. Every situation can be cracked open on the inside, reconfigured in a different regime of perception and signification, altering the landscape of what can be seen and what can be thought, along with the field of the possible and the distribution of capacities and incapacities. The method of equality is at work everywhere at any time. It is true that it promises no definite future. But new horizons are not defined by the planning of the future. On the contrary, it is from the division at work in the present, from the inventions of the method of equality, that unpredictable futures can emerge.

seven

# OF THE POVERTY OF OUR LIBERTY

## The Greatness and Limits of Hegel's Doctrine of Ethical Life

AXEL HONNETH

NO OTHER normative ideal appears more self-evident or attractive to us today than the idea of individual freedom. Simply reading the daily newspaper, as Hegel did, will leave us without any doubt about the contemporary importance of this value, both for the motivation and for the justification of social action. References to the priority of individual freedom are found in the platforms of nearly all political parties; they serve to justify structural interventions in the labor market as well as legal reforms; they are invoked to initiate social movements and even to explain far-reaching decisions in the personal sphere. To be sure, when freedom is invoked in these ways it is usually supplemented by further values that figure either as facilitating conditions or—more rarely—as the ends of liberty. It is said by some, for example, that freedom can exist only among equals, or that it presupposes security, and that therefore equality or security are necessary preconditions of freedom. Others say that love requires uncoerced and voluntary affection, and that individual freedom therefore is valued for the sake of love and as its prerequisite. But in these and similar arguments, freedom remains the key concept in that without it the other values would either lose their significance altogether or retain an appeal that would be normatively unintelligible. Considering what a central place the value of individual freedom occupies in our cultural and social self-understanding, it is bound to strike us as surprising how unsure we remain about its conceptual import in social contexts. Public discourse about freedom tends to treat it as though it possessed some singular mode of realization, even as we know and can in fact literally see that there are profound differences between, say, the freedom of political speech, the freedom of contract in the labor market, and the freedom of spontaneous association in a romantic relationship.

So far, none of the efforts philosophers have made to remedy this situation by means of conceptual distinctions between different forms of freedom has met their self-avowed goal. This is especially true of Isaiah Berlin's famous distinction between negative and positive liberty, which succeeded at generating some philosophical excitement but has been unable to supply us—insofar as we aim at self-understanding—with a sufficiently fine-grained clarification, if only because the phenomenology of positive liberty remained too vague and given to misunderstanding.[1] I am going to argue that even today Hegel's doctrine of ethical life represents a superior and more persuasive alternative. It is a philosophical source that can still elucidate the concept of freedom for us as it is practiced and valued by us. He assigned this conception the theoretical function of teaching the members of modern societies about the need to differentiate between distinct exercises of liberty (I will set aside the numerous other purposes that Hegel's conception of modern ethical life was meant to serve, which I will return to). Indeed, the theory of the free will that he offers in his *Philosophy of Right* can be seen as an explanation of how to distinguish different forms of individual liberty in such a way that they can then be respectively assigned their proper place in the institutional framework of functionally complex modern societies. My procedure will be as follows: First, I will explain to what extent the doctrine of ethical life that Hegel develops in his *Philosophy of Right* is meant to lay out distinctions between different forms of freedom. That in itself is no easy task, since the primary purpose of Hegel's idea of ethical life seems to be to identify a sphere of institutional reliability that is immune to the continuous questioning and reflection in which modern, "free" subjects are engaged. The connection between the idea of ethical life and human freedom is therefore not an obvious one. In a second step, I will show how Hegel proceeds from his theory of the will to identifying a variety of distinct forms of individual freedom within the sphere of modern ethical life. Here we need to ask ourselves whether we are in fact justified in supposing that Hegel's theory of ethical life still retains the power, for us today, to bring some order into the conceptions of freedom that we practice and aspire to, and to assign each of them a distinct institutional place. Finally, we should recognize that Hegel's doctrine of ethical life suffers from certain deficits, largely resulting from the fact that he does not always follow through with his own fundamental intentions. In a third step, I will turn to these limitations of his doctrine of ethical life, and I will raise the question once more of his contemporary relevance.

* * *

Just as he does throughout his *Realphilosophie*—that is to say, that part of his mature system devoted to an explanation of "actuality"—so too in his theory of right and of the state, in his theory of "objective spirit," Hegel introduces his operative concepts in two registers: first, in a register of logical determinations, and second, in a register that is closer to a descriptive grasp of the phenomena. This twofold conceptual apparatus remains one of the most attractive features of Hegel's project. As Dieter Henrich has remarked,[2] one of Hegel's greatest talents lay in his ability to counterbalance his efforts at delivering a formal-ontological analysis of reality by identifying closely corresponding features of our natural and social environment in a way that allows even a reader unacquainted with Hegel's *Logic* to follow the course of the argument. His ability to think in a way that is at once highly abstract and diagnostically concrete renders Hegel a sociologist avant la lettre. Before this discipline even existed, Hegel showed himself to be a great and nearly unsurpassed social theorist of modernity.



When we aim to understand the intention and purpose of the idea of "ethical life," we can make use of this double meaning of all the terms employed by Hegel in his *Realphilosophie*. In its logical guise, Hegel's philosophy of right and of the state is an attempt to describe the process of the realization or self-actualization of the determinations of reason insofar as those determinations have resulted in a certain objective social reality.[3] In its phenomenological or empirical guise, Hegel's aim is to bring to our awareness those phenomena of our social existence that show us to be the sons and daughters of modernity insofar as we actively participate, through our practices, in generating the rational determinations that characterize our society. If one wanted to invoke an influential contemporary view in social theory to bolster Hegel's intentions, one might say that Hegel wants to emphasize those among our "collective" ascriptions of status functions that correspond to general, quasi-organic properties of reason.[4] Now as we know, Hegel's two-sided analysis of modern society presupposes that a long process of historical development has already taken place—a process that has first made it the case that at this point in time, that is to say, around 1800, we can take for granted the existence of institutional arrangements that reflect the determinations of reason. If we wish to understand the intention behind Hegel's philosophy of right and of the state, we should therefore bear in mind that the social reality of which it offers an account is one that has already attained a degree of rationality such that its social practices and institutions can be considered embodiments of the logical determinations of spirit.[5]

This presupposition, which is central to his *Philosophy of Right* as a whole, follows from the fact—which Hegel presents as nearly obvious—that it was only the transition to modernity that placed social institutions under the demand to realize individual freedom. In modernity it is no longer just the individual with his or her particular aspirations and beliefs who can be thought of as free. Rather, the functionally necessary social institutions themselves are now considered as making possible the realization of freedom in the external domain of social action.[6] In his *Philosophy of History* especially, Hegel explains why only such transition in the meaning and scope of freedom, from the merely internal sphere to the objective world of social institutions, allows the logical determinations of spirit to find full application. Hegel shows how each successive stage in the world-historical process extends the scope of social reality. This process can be thought of as the realization of the self-referring subjectivity of spirit, since each further step eliminates a piece of that opaque, still spiritless objectivity that evades all attempts at grasping it in terms of logical determinations. Not until the "new epoch" of modernity when freedom has become the organizing principle of all the central social institutions is it possible to fully express social reality in terms of logical concepts. For only then is it the case that in relating to their social institutions, individuals at the same time relate to themselves in just the way that is required by Hegel's conception of spirit as a self-relating type of organism.[7] Thus Hegel's philosophy of history delivers the premises on whose basis Hegel can then build his *Philosophy of Right* as a formal-ontological account of social reality: all the aspects of modern societies that need to be considered inasmuch as they are displaying the "actuality" of freedom must conform to the concepts of a "logic" that seeks to describe spirit in the process of its undiminished self-actualization.[8]

With regard to the point of departure of Hegel's *Philosophy of Right*, these presuppositions entail that right from the beginning the canonical modern concept of freedom needs to be explicated in a way that allows us to recognize in it the features of spirit in its process of self-relation. If the kind of freedom that is supposed to have attained actuality in modern societies did not lend itself to being understood along these lines, it would be unintelligible how one could develop a theory of these modern societies according to the determinations of logic. Hegel meets this challenge in his introduction, which constitutes a fascinating attempt to wrest the concept of freedom from the hands of the prevailing doctrines of his day, at the same time considerably expanding the range of the tasks faced by any "philosophy of right."[9] Hegel's line of argument is highly complex and traverses several stages of determination. I will provide only a very basic description of it, since my goal here is mainly to explain the point of departure of the idea of "ethical life." Hegel sets out from a conception of freedom that is rather simplistic but very influential in modern society. According to this conception, an individual subject is "free" to the extent that there is a certain external space within which his activity can unfold without any interventions by other subjects. It is inconsequential, from this perspective, whether the goals that the subject is able to realize within this space can in turn be described as "free"—that is to say, whether those purposes arise from what are regarded as good reasons, rather than simply from natural causes. All that the conception is interested in is the possibility of realizing arbitrary goals without outside interference.[10] This formulation already indicates that what Hegel has in mind here is roughly what Isaiah Berlin much later was to call "negative liberty": that is to say, a type of individual freedom that an individual is supposed to enjoy simply by virtue of being granted a circumscribed space for the unhindered pursuit of his goals. It is not difficult to see why in Hegel's view this conception must be rejected as insufficient. It does not even approximate Hegel's master concept of "spirit," since nothing guarantees that the individual purposes whose unhindered realization is being enabled are themselves something "spiritual," rather than simply part of the causal order.[11] For Hegel it is impossible to speak of "freedom" in any demanding or meaningful sense as long as we do not know whether an individual's intentions themselves qualify as free. Yet as we will see, he incorporates this still primitive conception into his own theory of social modernity and assigns it a place within the subsystem of "abstract right," since he is convinced that without it we cannot make sense of our own institutionalized practices as ones in which freedom is in fact actualized.

There is a second conception of freedom that Hegel discusses in his introduction because of its powerful presence in our modern self-understanding. In contrast with the first conception, the focus is here shifted entirely to the goals or intentions whose external realization is at issue. On this second model, which Isaiah Berlin would have classified as a "positive" concept of liberty, human actions can properly be called free only if they proceed from purposes that transcend mere natural causality and are instead anchored in self-posited or subjectively endorsed reasons.[12] In Hegel's view there can be no doubt that this constitutes a major advance over the merely external concept of negative liberty. The idea that freedom requires rational self-determination brings the whole concept closer to that of spirit, which after all consists in a reflexive self-relation. But a comparison with the structure of spirit also shows why this second concept of positive or reflexive freedom, which is largely derived from Kant, must still appear deficient to Hegel. To put the point in terms of Hegel's philosophy of spirit, this concept remains deficient because it lacks the moment of objectivity that spirit must possess insofar as it conceives even of its own other—that is to say, nonspirit or the realm of the object—as a product of its own reflexive relation to itself.[13] Translating this into the more concrete, phenomenological vocabulary that Hegel employs throughout to bring out the correspondences between his logical determinations and the familiar features of our environment, his critique of the idea of freedom as rational self-determination is that it conceives of individual freedom as though it was enough for us to have rational intentions, ones supported by good reasons, whereas in fact everything depends on whether we can think of the reality with which we are confronted as already being *itself* an emanation or embodiment of a process of self-determination.

Thus Hegel's introduction yields the difficult task of delineating a third concept of freedom, one that mirrors the structure of spirit by allowing us to think of the objectivity of social reality as a product of the activity of rational, self-relating subjects.[14] At this point, it comes as no surprise that Hegel's concept of "ethical life" is meant to meet exactly this challenge.[15] In explaining this notion, it is advisable to start by attending to the more intuitive formulations that Hegel offers to show that his logical concepts can be translated into the language of everyday phenomena. Thus when Hegel tries to explain what it could mean to say that freedom should be thought of as a subjectivity that knows itself to be spontaneous and active in its very object, he immediately points to the concrete examples of "friendship" and "love." "Here," writes Hegel, "we are not one-sidedly within ourselves, but willingly limit ourselves with reference to another, even while knowing ourselves in this limitation as ourselves. In this determinacy, the human being should not feel determined; on the contrary, he attains his self-awareness only by regarding the other as other. Thus, freedom lies neither in indeterminacy nor in determinacy, but is both at once."[16] What Hegel here calls "self-limitation" may be thought of, at the level of human psychology, as a predecessor of the kind of rational self-determination that the second, Kantian model took to be the decisive mark of individual freedom. When I decide to enter into a friendship or a loving relationship, I am not blindly following my inclinations but am guided by certain considerations and reasons; and to the extent that those reasons persuade me of the rightness of my action, they amount to a source of rational self-determination, which here consists in a limitation of my motives to what the relationship permits. But Hegel's concern is to point out that this idea of a self-limitation resulting from autonomy is one-sided and misleading, since in friendship and love my experience is precisely that the other person is a condition of my realizing my own, self-chosen ends. In cases like this, where what the other person desires from me is what I desire from him, it is more appropriate to speak of self-*release* than to speak of self-limitation, since that to which I relate is here something that first completes my freedom.

When we now try to translate these concrete clues provided by Hegel back into the formal terminology of his theory of spirit, we already have the key to a rough understanding of his third concept of freedom, which he characterizes as "objective." In relations of friendship and love, a subject is reflexively related to himself in such a way that he recognizes the objectivity of the other person as a reflection of his own intentions and in that sense as his own other. Thus when we abstract from the special cases of friendship and love, we can say with Hegel that objective freedom is found wherever social routines and institutionalized practices allow subjects to view the intentions of those with whom they interact as objective embodiments of their own, reflexively constituted ends.[17] Only in this way does the subjectivity of individual agents attain a shape that is analogous to the more encompassing form of spirit, in that they can recognize the objectivity of those institutionalized practices as the product of their own reflexive self-determination. All those practices that reliably offer subjects the opportunity to make this kind of experience are classified by Hegel as belonging to the part of social reality he calls "ethical life." Ethical life is superior to other institutional structures of social reality not simply because it relieves individuals of the burden of choice or reflection, but because it allows them a kind of freedom that far surpasses the other freedoms cherished by modernity, in that it affords a much more profound and saturated experience of the absence of constraint. By now I need hardly add that in Hegel's eyes, one indication of this superiority of ethical life vis-à-vis other conceptions of freedom is the fact that it alone can be expressed in terms of the logical concepts of spirit. For while the forms of activity associated with the two other types of freedom retain a residue of inscrutable, utterly alien objectivity, which makes it impossible to fully explicate them in terms of the structure of spirit, no such obstacles remain at the stage of objective, ethically mediated freedom, since subjects are here in a position to view the object as their own other, which is to say, as a product of their own self-relation.

From this intermediate conclusion, Hegel needs to take only a small further step to be able to present the full program of his *Philosophy of Right* and thus his own particular idea of "right"; and only at that point can we properly understand what Hegel is aiming at with his distinction between different conceptions of freedom as I have just sketched it. Hegel here proceeds in a strictly immanent fashion. First, he shows how the philosophy of right as practiced by his contemporaries routinely starts out from a concept of individual freedom and reasons from it to conclusions about the individual rights that should be protected by the state. By this methodology, the extent and content of subjective rights that the state should safeguard will depend on whether a "negative" or a "positive" conception of free will is being presupposed. Hegel's ingenious next step is to demonstrate that if we derive our conception of rights in this way, we end up being forced to give up our starting idea of merely subjective rights as soon as we decide to rely on the objective conception of freedom, rather than on one of the two deficient conceptions. Once we think of a subject's freedom, properly speaking, as consisting neither in a defined space of arbitrary choice nor (following Kant) in reflexive self-determination, but rather as a matter of participating and collaborating in ethical institutions, the idea of right itself needs to be expanded, since those institutions themselves are now accorded a normatively grounded right to existence.[18] We might say that Hegel seizes from the traditional philosophy of right *its* own concept of right by demonstrating that this concept has to contain not just subjective claims but also social facts and, more specifically, certain kinds of institutions, once the guiding principle of individual freedom is conceived in an adequate way—which is to say, along the lines of objective freedom. The generally accepted definition of right, says Hegel, "embodies the view, especially prevalent since Rousseau, according to which the substantial basis and primary factor is supposed to be not the will [of the individual] as a rational will that has being in and for itself, or the spirit as *true* spirit, but will and spirit as the *particular* individual, as the will of the single person in his distinctive arbitrariness."[19] We can continue the thought as follows: when the free will of the individual is instead modeled on spirit, as a self-relating will that recognizes itself in the objectivity of specific practices, the definition of right must change too, since it now has to incorporate the institutionalized practices that make this kind of self-relation possible.

Hegel's *Philosophy of Right* executes the program just outlined. It relies on an extended, social-ontological concept of right in order to show that all those institutional practices in which modern subjects can experience an objectively mediated self-relation exist rightfully, in that they are spheres of action justified by the requirements of individual freedom. My next step will be to show that Hegel's approach pushes him to further distinguish between different shapes of objective freedom itself, each associated with one particular set of institutions. My goal is to argue for the continuing relevance of Hegel's theory of ethical life by showing that it supplies us with a normative vocabulary that we can use to assess the respective value of the various freedoms we practice.

* * *

As we have seen, Hegel's concept of "ethical life" is meant to identify those among our social institutions that allow interacting subjects to experience a kind of freedom that is not merely negative or reflective but rather objective. By "objective freedom" Hegel means a type of individual freedom that enables the individual to recognize himself in institutionalized practices, in the sense that he views the habitualized intentions of those with whom he interacts as preconditions and even as products of his own rationally generated intentions. But before Hegel can proceed to decorate the relevant social institutions or practices with the title "ethical," he first needs to solve a difficult problem that arises from the claim of a "philosophy of right" to deliver an analysis of the objective institutional conditions of freedom that is equally applicable to all members of modern societies. This claim entails that Hegel cannot rest content with pointing to some particular intentions that meet the criterion of rational self-determination. Rather, he has to prove something far more demanding: first, that in the modern age there are certain ends that are shared by all rational subjects, and second, that they can realize those ends, or satisfy their purposes, only by participating in intersubjective practices that are the outcomes of prior historical developments. Now unfortunately, Hegel did not go to the length of successively arguing for these two distinct claims. As in all of his work, the crucial line of argument is dressed up as a derivation grounded in his philosophy of spirit, where the conceptual steps that are intuitively accessible to us are barely separable from Hegel's logical determinations. When we try nonetheless to enact such a separation in retrospect, we can say roughly the following about the exoteric side of Hegel's argument, the side that makes contact with our concrete experience: in contrast with Kant, Hegel is convinced that in rationally determining himself, an individual is usually guided by those normative rules that he has come to know, through a process of socialization, as patterns manifested in the institutions that surround him. For such an individual, it would be wrongheaded to proceed as though he had an arbitrary plurality of ends that he now personally needs to test for their moral rightness. Instead, we as rationally self-determining beings usually rely on our mutual agreement to conform our activity to the maxims embodied in those practices within whose moral horizon we have grown up.[20] Hegel's view is that this allows us to assume that insofar as they are self-transparent and rational subjects, his contemporaries share as many purposes or intentions as there are institutional structures that have formed them as individual spirits through practices that invite rational consent. In short, the task of Hegel's doctrine of ethical life is to identify those general, motivationally formative institutions of his time that enable each one of their members to recognize in the intentions of the others an objectivity of his own freedom.

It speaks to the greatness of Hegel's gifts as a sociologist that he solves this problem in a way whose detailed execution may no longer be fully tenable, but whose general theoretical structure remains sound even today. If we consider similarly ambitious proposals in social theory that were developed much later, for example, those of Durkheim and Talcott Parsons, we can see that they make no fundamental advances over the distinctions that Hegel laid out in his *Philosophy of Right*.[21] In his younger years, Hegel enthusiastically pursued the idea that even complex societies could achieve the required degree of integration through an extension of relations of love and friendship. Once he gave up on this thought, he developed the much more realistic view—not least thanks to his study of the contemporary theories of political economy—that the reproduction of modern societies depends on the joint operation of three general, motivationally formative sets of institutions. The first of these, personal relations based on love and friendship, retains elements of his earlier conception; but on his revised view, it is now supplemented by the capitalist market economy and by the political institutions of a constitutional monarchy.[22] Yet Hegel's path toward his mature philosophy did not leave him so disenchanted as to abandon the project of modeling all three of these spheres of institutionalized action on the structure of reciprocity that had originally been restricted to relations of love alone. And this project, in turn, set him the task that we already saw elaborated in the introduction with respect to the case of love and friendship, namely, to identify in the other two institutional spheres, the market and the state, the substance of "objective freedom," which is to say, the peculiar mechanism whereby individuals mutually encounter their own self-determined purposes as objectively given in the other's activity. By following down this path, Hegel was eventually led to the conviction, which is central to his *Philosophy of Right* as a whole, that the three modern institutions of love (now conceived as romantic love), of a socially embedded market, and of a monarchic yet civic state constituted spheres of ethical life. By being molded by the moral language of these three sets of institutions, he thought, and by exercising their capacity for self-determination, individuals would adopt ends and intentions reasonably directed at those institutions, and they would then be able to view the satisfaction of those intentions in the corresponding practices as amounting to an unconstrained objective realization of their own individual freedom.

Now it is of course not sufficient for Hegel simply to list these three forms of objective freedom side by side. In order to be able to properly individuate and describe them, he needs to show how they fit together in a normatively structured ordering that allows us to compare them and assess their respective value. In ordering or ranking them in such a way, Hegel draws again on his quasi-organic concept of spirit. He now applies it to the three institutionalized spheres of freedom, just as he had earlier relied on it in surveying and evaluating current conceptions of individual freedom, and we should therefore expect that the different shapes of objective freedom are more complete and hence more valuable the less they involve any residual elements of natural causality. In its most complete realization, objective freedom should then fully conform to the model of spirit, which recognizes itself as reflected in its objectivity and therefore knows no external constraints. Here again one is impressed by how masterfully Hegel manages to bring his purely logical determinations to bear on an account of social reality that is both illuminating and empirically plausible. Thus the practices of reciprocal caring and affection found in relations of love and friendship and within the family represent a subordinate stage of objective freedom since what is satisfied in them is merely our socially interpreted but in the end still natural needs.[23] The money-mediated practices of exchanging goods and services that are institutionalized in the capitalist market embody a higher degree of objective freedom, since the individual interests operative in them are already informed by prudential reflection.[24] And the practices of caring for the common good and of standing up for one another for which the monarchic-civic state makes room constitute the highest form of objective freedom, because the intentions that attain their objective existence in them have shed the last remnants of natural determination and express purely spiritual, rationally formed attitudes.[25] I am not claiming that these specific ways of characterizing the different sets of practices are flawless, or were so at least in Hegel's own time. As we know, Hegel's depiction of romantic love and of the familial relations based on it was guided by the patriarchal prejudices of his own day;[26] and his description of the state completely loses sight of the fact that by the terms of his own project this should be a matter of symmetrical relations among citizens, who are able to reciprocally recognize their honorable actions as objective realizations of their own respective efforts.[27] But the basic idea of this tripartite conception of ethical life was in his time, and remains today, an imposing challenge to the modern conception of freedom. It forces us to give serious thought to the question whether we might not be more free if we come to think of institutions and practices not as restrictions on or presuppositions of a merely subjective freedom, but rather as themselves embodying a type of communicative freedom. In its design and its basic conceptual structure, Hegel's theory of ethical life already contains all the necessary resources for extending our understanding of freedom. Hegel distinguished between needs (including bodily needs), instrumentally rational interests, and individual self-valuation as the three sources of those intentions that can be freely satisfied only through institutionalized reciprocity and that thereby afford a sense of enhanced freedom. He sought to explain that this kind of intersubjective reciprocity is possible in principle only among equals. And finally, he already described in outline the specific types of institutions that would make room for these shapes of ethical, social, or communicative freedom. But nowhere in the *Philosophy of Right* do we find any hints of whether or how the institutions he envisaged might one day undergo further developments that would make them more amenable to the basic demand for relations of reciprocity among equals. Instead, he treated as sacrosanct those particular arrangements of family, market, and state that a very charitable interpretation might have found to be in existence in his day, and he failed to so much as consider the possibility that they might exhibit an inner dynamic, a conflict-fueled, immanent progressive tendency.

This conservatism of Hegel's social analysis reflects a quite serious flaw in the construction of his theory of ethical life, to which I will now briefly turn.

* * *

I have already indicated that Hegel by no means wanted to banish the deficient forms of individual freedom from his theory of right and state. He was enough of a liberal to recognize that the existence of purely private opportunities to draw personal boundaries and engage in ethical reflection is a constitutive feature of modern societies. After the introduction to the *Philosophy of Right* laid open the deficiencies of a merely negative conception of freedom and of the idea of individual self-determination, both reappear in the main part of the book under different names, which now designate two spheres of activity that have in fact long been part of social reality. Under the heading "abstract right," Hegel subsumes the liberal rights that had been established in rudimentary form by the time he was writing and that were meant to ensure that each adult individual's life, property, and freedom of contract would be protected by the state.[28] By "morality," on the other hand, Hegel meant each individual's institutionally protected chance to insist for moral reasons on his own conception of what is right.[29] Even though these two institutions precede the objective, ethical forms of freedom in Hegel's order of presentation, this should not lead us to conclude that he thought of them merely as preliminary entry conditions for participation in the social practices of family, market, and state—as though individuals would, as it were, lay aside their individual rights and their moral autonomy once personal reflection on those rights and on the verdicts of their conscience had convinced them to take part in the institutions of intersubjective reciprocity. Rather, Hegel assumes that liberal rights and the chance for moral self-positioning continue to form the backdrop of all interactions in the three ethical spheres, in that they allow individuals in principle to withdraw from practical commitments or to morally object to them. It therefore remains constitutive of the sphere of ethical life as a whole that the members of a society should have permanent access to the two options that Albert Hirschman called "exit" and "voice," that is to say, the options of voluntary withdrawal and of morally articulated protest.[30]

This inclusion of "subjective" liberties in the concept of institutionalized ethical life already introduces a dynamic element of openness and transgression into Hegel's theory, which his presentation is unable to fully keep in check. For nothing in Hegel's description rules out the possibility that individual objections may at one point add up to a collective protest that could call into question the very constitution of the ethical institutions themselves. It is true that Hegel sometimes mentions the possibility of such a collective "outrage," especially in his analysis of the capitalist market;[31] but he does not countenance the fact that this entails a dynamization of the specific kind of ethical life favored by him. Doing so, after all, would have meant leaving the adequacy of his own theory of right and state vulnerable to the conflictual, even revolutionary changes that might in the future result from the frictions that Hegel himself allowed to be a feature of the system of institutionalized freedoms. As we know, Hegel did not take this further step. He did not regard his *Philosophy of Right* as an intermediate stage in the process whereby modern society accounts for its own potential for freedom. Rather, he took it to have a conclusive character: from the vantage point of an institutionally embodied and, in this very embodiment, self-comprehending spirit, his theory was meant to show how objective freedom had once and for all found a secure foothold in the institutions of the family, the market, and the state. For those of us who look back at Hegel's theory of ethical life after almost two hundred years, history has taught us otherwise: the forces of individualization and of autonomy and the potential included in negative and reflective freedom have released a dynamic that has affected the system of ethical life itself and that has left none of its institutions in the exact normative position that Hegel had once assigned to them. For this reason, Hegel's *Philosophy of Right* can no longer serve today as a theory of social freedom with respect to its concrete execution but only with respect to its outlines and its general plan of construction. We can learn from it how poor our freedoms are if we try to comprehend them purely in terms of subjective rights, moral autonomy, or some combination of the two. Following Hegel would lead us to insist on the fact that individual freedom in social contexts has to mean first and foremost the experience of an absence of constraint and of personal development, resulting from the fact that our own individual but generalizable goals are advanced by the equally general goals of others.

But once we regard this kind of "objective"—or, as we might now rather call it, "social"—freedom as the core of our entire conception of freedom, in relation to which the previous ideas of freedom possess only a derivative status, we must also draw the same consequence Hegel did and revise our familiar conception of justice. What we consider "just" in the highly developed societies of our own time should no longer be taken to depend simply on whether and to what extent all members of a society enjoy negative and reflective freedom. Rather, what we consider to be "just" is subject to the further condition that these individuals are equally able to participate in the institutionalized spheres of reciprocity, that is to say, in families and personal relations, in the labor market, and in the process of democratic decision-making. It then becomes central to the idea of social justice that those normatively weighty and therefore "ethical" institutions require legal protection, state oversight, and the support of civil society in order to be able to realize the claim to social freedom that underlies them. Only a division of labor and the interplay between the law, political institutions, and a solidarity-fostering public sphere can sustain the institutional structures to which the members of a society owe the multiple facets of their interlocking freedoms, and to which as a result we all owe a culture of freedom.

# NOTES

## 1. JACQUES RANCIÈRE AND AXEL HONNETH: TWO CRITICAL APPROACHES TO THE POLITICAL

I would like to thank John Abromeit and Jean-Philippe Deranty for their helpful reading and comments.

1. The most recent is Oliver Davis, *Jacques Rancière* (Cambridge: Polity, 2010), 96–98. Previously, see Jean-Philippe Deranty, "Mésentente et Reconnaissance: Honneth face à Rancière," in *Où en est la Théorie Critique?*, ed. Emmanuel Renault and Yves Sintomer (Paris: La Découverte, 2003), 185–199; Deranty, "Jacques Rancière's Contribution to the Ethics of Recognition," *Political Theory* 31, no. 1 (2003): 136–156. On Honneth, see Jean-Philippe Deranty and Emmanuel Renault, "Politicising Honneth's Ethics of Recognition," *Thesis Eleven* 88 (2007): 92–111.
2. Jacques Rancière, *Disagreement: Politics and Philosophy*, trans. Julie Rose (Minneapolis: University of Minnesota Press, 1998); originally *La Mésentente: Politique et philosophie* (Paris: Galilée, 1995); Axel Honneth, *The Struggle for Recognition: The Moral Grammar of Social Conflicts*, trans. Joel Anderson (Cambridge: Polity, 1994); originally *Kampf um Anerkennung: Zur moralischen Grammatik sozialer Konflikte* (Frankfurt: Suhrkamp, 1992).
3. Max Horkheimer, "Traditional and Critical Theory," in *Critical Theory: Selected Essays*, trans. Matthew J. O'Connell and others (New York: Continuum, 2002), 188–243. A critical theory of society is "a theory dominated at every turn by a concern for reasonable conditions of life" (199). It considers the "world which is given to the individual and which he must accept and take into account" as being, "in its present and continuing form,

a product of the activity of society as a whole" (200), though the individual sees it as a given imposed on its will from outside. In opposition to traditional theory, critical theory aims at the "transformation of society as a whole" through the "intensification of the struggle with which the theory is connected" (219), for society to be the result of the "conscious spontaneity" of "free individuals." See also Max Horkheimer, *Between Philosophy and Social Science*, trans. F. Hunter, M. Kramer, and J. Torpey (Cambridge, Mass.: MIT Press, 1993).

4. Theodor W. Adorno and Max Horkheimer, *Dialectic of Enlightenment*, trans. Edmund Jephcott (Stanford: Stanford University Press, 2002); Theodor W. Adorno, *Negative Dialectics*, trans. E. B. Ashton (London: Routledge, 1973).
5. Louis Althusser, "Ideology and State Apparatuses: Notes Towards an Investigation," in *Lenin and Philosophy, and Other Essays*, trans. Ben Brewster (New York: Monthly Review Press, 1971); Michel Foucault, "What Is Enlightenment?," in *The Foucault Reader*, ed. Paul Rabinow (New York: Pantheon, 1984), 32–50; Foucault, "What Is Critique?," in *The Politics of Truth*, ed. Sylvere Lotringer (Los Angeles: Semiotext[e], 2007), 41–81; Jean-François Lyotard, *The Postmodern Condition: A Report on Knowledge* (Minneapolis: University of Minnesota Press, 1984); Lyotard, *The Differend: Phrases in Dispute* (Minneapolis: University of Minnesota Press, 1989); Gilles Deleuze and Felix Guattari, *Kafka: Towards a Minor Literature*, trans. Dana Polan (Minneapolis: University of Minnesota Press, 1986); Deleuze and Guattari, *A Thousand Plateaus: Capitalism and Schizophrenia*, trans. Brian Massumi (Minneapolis: University of Minnesota Press, 1987); Jacques Derrida, *Of Grammatology*, trans. Gayatri Chakravorty Spivak (Baltimore: Johns Hopkins University Press, 1978); Derrida, *Writing and Difference*, trans. Alan Bass (Chicago: University of Chicago Press, 1978); Alain Badiou, *Metapolitics*, trans. Jason Barker (New York: Verso, 2005); Badiou, *Being and Event*, trans. Oliver Feltham (New York: Continuum, 2005); Étienne Balibar, *Masses, Classes, Ideas: Studies on Politics and Philosophy Before and After Marx*, trans. James Swenson (New York: Routledge, 1994); Judith Butler, Ernesto Laclau, and Slavoj Žižek, *Contingency, Hegemony, Universality: Contemporary Dialogues on the Left* (London: Verso, 2000); Judith Butler, *The Psychic Life of Power: Subjection in Theories* (Stanford: Stanford University Press, 1997); Judith Butler, "*What Is Critique?* An Essay on Foucault's Virtue," in *The Political*, ed. David Ingram (Oxford: Blackwell, 2002), 212–226. See also Jon Simons,

ed., *Contemporary Critical Theorists: From Lacan to Said* (Edinburgh: Edinburgh University Press, 2004); Simons, ed., *Contemporary Critical Theorists: From Agamben to Žižek* (Edinburgh: Edinburgh University Press, 2010).

6. Foucault, "What Is Enlightenment?," 32–50; Foucault, "*Omnes et Singulatim*: Towards a Critique of Political Reason," *Tanner Lectures on Human Values*, vol. 2, ed. Sterling M. McMurrin (Cambridge: Cambridge University Press, 1981); Foucault, "The Subject and Power," in *Michel Foucault: Beyond Structuralism and Hermeneutics*, ed. Hubert Dreyfus and Paul Rabinow (Chicago: University of Chicago Press, 1982), 208–226.
7. Foucault, "What Is Enlightenment?," 50.
8. Axel Honneth, *Pathologies of Reason: On the Legacy of Critical Theory* (New York: Columbia University Press, 2009).
9. Honneth, *The Struggle for Recognition*; Honneth, *Suffering from Indeterminacy: An Attempt at a Reactualization of Hegel's Philosophy of Right: Two Lectures*, Spinoza Lectures (Amsterdam: Uitgeverij Van Gorcum, 2000); Honneth, *Freedom's Right* (New York: Columbia University Press, 2014).
10. Axel Honneth, "Domination and Moral Struggle: The Philosophical Heritage of Marxism Revisited," in *Fragmented World of the Social: Essays in Social and Political Philosophy*, ed. Charles W. Wright (New York: State University of New York Press, 1995), 3–14. On his distance to Marx, see Jean-Philippe Deranty, "Les horizons marxistes de éthique de la reconnaissance," *Actuel Marx* 38 (2005): 159–178; Deranty, "Repressed Materiality: Retrieving the Materialism in Axel Honneth's *Theory of Recognition*," in *Recognition, Work, Politics: New Directions in French Critical Theory*, ed. Jean-Philippe Deranty et al. (Leiden: Brill, 2007), 137–164; Deranty, "Critique of Political Economy and Contemporary Critical Theory: A Defence of Honneth's Theory of Recognition," in *The Philosophy of Recognition: Historical and Contemporary Perspectives*, ed. Hans-Christoph Schmidt-am-Busch and Christopher F. Zurn (Berlin: Akademie Verlag, 2009).
11. He distinguishes an inner circle (Adorno, Horkheimer, and Marcuse) and a periphery (Neumann, Kirchheimer, Fromm, and Benjamin) of the Frankfurt School in Axel Honneth, "Critical Theory," in *The Fragmented World of the Social*, 61–91.
12. To recall the core diagnostic concepts used in this tradition to express social negativity, Horkheimer spoke of an "irrational organization" of society. Adorno later analyzed the "administrated world." Marcuse used

concepts such as "one-dimensional society" or "repressive tolerance." And finally Habermas used the formula "colonization of the life-world." Axel Honneth, "A Social Pathology of Reason: On the Intellectual Legacy of Critical Theory," in *Pathologies of Reason*, 19–42.

13. Ibid., 20.
14. Ibid., 30.
15. Ibid., 42.
16. Axel Honneth, *Critique of Power: Reflective Stages in a Critical Social Theory*, trans. Kenneth Baynes (Cambridge, Mass.: MIT Press, 1991).
17. On the relation of Rancière to Marx (through Althusser), see Emmanuel Renault, "The Many Marx of Jacques Rancière," in *Jacques Rancière and the Contemporary Scene: The Philosophy of Radical Equality*, ed. Jean-Philippe Deranty and Alison Ross (New York: Continuum, 2012), 167–186.
18. Karl Marx, *Capital*, vol. 1, trans. Ben Fowkes (London: Penguin, 1990). Rancière participated with Althusser in the book *Lire le Capital*, by Louis Althusser, Roger Establet, Pierre Macherey, and Étienne Balibar (Paris: Presses Universitaires de France, 1996); translated as *Reading Capital*, trans. Ben Brewster (London: Verso, 2009).
19. Jacques Rancière, *Proletarian Nights: The Workers' Dream in Nineteenth-Century France*, trans. John Drury (London: Verso, 2012).
20. Ibid., vii.
21. Ibid., viii.
22. In this book, he relies on a concept of identity from which he will later distance himself. See chapter 2 of this volume, especially pp. 38–41.
23. Althusser, "Ideology and State Apparatuses."
24. Jacques Rancière, *The Ignorant Schoolmaster: Five Lessons in Intellectual Emancipation*, trans. Kristin Ross (Stanford: Stanford University Press, 1991).
25. It is the definition given by Jacques Rancière in "Biopolitics or Politics?," in *Dissensus: On Politics and Aesthetics*, trans. Steven Corcoran (New York: Continuum, 2010), 91–95.
26. Jacques Rancière, "The Rationality of Disagreement," in *Disagreement*, 43–60.
27. Ibid., 44.
28. See Axel Honneth, *The Struggle for Recognition*, and the exchange with Nancy Fraser: Honneth and Fraser, *Redistribution or Recognition? A Political-Philosophical Exchange*, trans. Joel Golb, James Ingram, and Christiane Wilke (London: Verso, 2003).

29. Jürgen Habermas, *Knowledge and Human Interests*, trans. Jeremy J. Shapiro (Cambridge: Polity, 1987), esp. the postscript.
30. Jürgen Habermas, *Between Facts and Norms*, trans. William Rehg (Cambridge: Polity, 1996). Such a criticism from Honneth to Habermas is developed in Emmanuel Renault, *L'expérience de l'injustice: Reconnaissance et clinique de l'injustice* (Paris: La Découverte, 2004).
31. See "Anerkennungsbeziehungen und Moral: Eine Diskussionsbemerkung zur anthropologischen *Erweiterung der Diskursethik*," in *Anthropologie, Ethik und Gesellschaft: Für Helmut Fahrenbach*, ed. Reinhard Brunner and Peter Kelbel (Frankfurt: Campus, 2000), 101–111.
32. Giovanna Borradori, *Philosophy in a Time of Terror: Dialogues with Jürgen Habermas and Jacques Derrida* (Chicago: University of Chicago Press, 2003).
33. Including on recognition: Axel Honneth "Grounding Recognition: A Rejoinder to Critical Questions," *Inquiry* 45 no. 4 (2002): 499–519.
34. Honneth and Fraser: *Redistribution or Recognition?* See also Fraser, "Rethinking Recognition," *New Left Review* 3 (2000): 107–120; and Fraser, "Recognition Without Ethics," *Theory, Culture and Society* 18, nos. 2–3 (2001): 21–42.
35. Joel Whitebook, "Mutual Recognition and the Work of the Negative," in *Pluralism and the Pragmatic Turn: The Transformation of Critical Theory, Essays in Honor of Thomas McCarthy*, ed. William Regh and James Bohman (Cambridge, Mass.: MIT Press, 2001), 257–291; Axel Honneth, "Facets of the Presocial Self: A Rejoinder to Joel Whitebook," in *The I and the We: Studies in the Theory of Recognition*, trans. Joseph Ganahl (Cambridge: Polity, 2012); Joel Whitebook, "Die Grenzen des *intersubjective turn*: Eine Erwiederung auf Axel Honneth," *Psyché: Zeitschrift für Psychoanalyse und ihre Anwendungen*, ed. Werner Bohleber, 3 (2003). See also Joel Whitebook, *Perversion and Utopia: A Study in Psychoanalysis and Critical Theory* (Cambridge, Mass.: MIT Press, 1995); Axel Honneth, "The Work of Negativity: A Psychoanalytical Revision of the Theory of Recognition," in *Recognition, Work, Politics: New Directions in French Critical Theory, Social and Critical Theory*, ed. Jean-Philippe Deranty, Danielle Petherbridge, John Rundell, and Robert Sinnerbrink (Boston: Brill, 2007); Axel Honneth, "Postmodern Identity and Object-Relations Theory: On the Seeming Obsolescence of Psychoanalysis," *Philosophical Explorations* 2, no. 3 (1999): 225–242.
36. Luc Boltanski, *On Critique: A Sociology of Emancipation* (Cambridge: Polity, 2011), which is the book made out of the lectures given during the

Adorno Vorlesungen in 2008 in Frankfurt on the invitation of Honneth; Luc Boltanski and Eve Chiapello, *The New Spirit of Capitalism*, trans. G. Elliott (London: Verso, 2007); Christophe Dejours, *Souffrance en France: La banalisation de l'injustice sociale* (Paris: Seuil, 1998).

37. Butler, Laclau, and Žižek, *Contingency, Hegemony, Universality*.
38. Judith Butler and Catherine Malabou, *Sois mon corps: Une lecture contemporaine de la domination et de la servitude chez Hegel* (Paris: Bayard, 2010).
39. Samantha Avenshen and David Owen, eds., *Foucault Contra Habermas: Recasting the Dialogue Between Genealogy and Critical Theory* (London: Sage, 1999); David Couzens Hoy and Thomas MacCarthy, *Critical Theory* (Oxford: Wiley-Blackwell, 1994); Michael Kelly, *Critique and Power: Recasting the Foucault/Habermas Debate*, Studies in Contemporary German Social Thought (Cambridge, Mass.: MIT Press, 1994). We can mention the edition by Axel Honneth and Martin Saar of *Michel Foucault: Zwischenbilanz einer Rezeption: Frankfurter Foucault Konferenz 2001* (Frankfurt: Suhrkamp Verlag, 2003). On critical theory, see Nikolas Kompridis, *Critique and Disclosure: Critical Theory Between Past and Future* (Cambridge, Mass.: MIT Press, 2006); and Michael Theunissen, "Society and History: A Critique of Critical Theory," in *Habermas: A Critical Reader*, ed. P. Dews (Oxford: Blackwell, 1999), 241–271.
40. Couzens Hoy and MacCarthy, *Critical Theory*, 2.
41. Axel Honneth, "Foucault and Adorno: Two Forms of the Critique of Modernity," in *Fragmented World of the Social*, 121–131. See also Axel Honneth, *Critique of Power*.
42. He underlines the difference between Adorno's account of the problematical character of modern individuality and Foucault's deconstruction of the subject.
43. Lasse Thomassen, ed., *The Derrida-Habermas Reader* (Chicago: University of Chicago, 2006).
44. Couzens Hoy and MacCarthy, *Critical Theory*, 4.
45. Jacques Rancière, *On the Shores of Politics*, trans. Liz Heron (London: Verso, 1995).
46. Lyotard, *The Differend*.
47. On Habermas and aesthetics, see, for example, Albrecht Wellmer, *The Persistence of Modernity: Essays on Aesthetics, Ethics and Postmodernism*, trans. David Midgley (Cambridge, Mass.: MIT Press, 1991); Pieter Duvenage, *Habermas and Aesthetics: The Limits of Communicative Reason* (Cambridge: Polity, 2003); David Colclasure, *Habermas and Literary Rationality*

(London: Routledge, 2010); Nicholas Hengen Fox, "A Habermasian Literary Criticism," *New Literary History* 43, no. 2 (2012): 235–254; Geoff Boucher, "The Politics of Aesthetic Affect: A Reconstruction of Habermas's Art Theory," *Parrhesia* 13 (2011): 62–78.

48. Jacques Rancière, *The Politics of Aesthetics: The Distribution of the Sensible*, trans. Gabriel Rockhill (New York: Continuum, 2006), 4.
49. Jacques Rancière, *Aesthetics and Its Discontents*, trans. Steve Corcoran (Cambridge: Polity, 2009).
50. Jacques Rancière, "The Ethical Turn of Aesthetics and Politics," trans. Jean-Philippe Deranty, *Critical Horizons* 7, no. 1 (2006); 1–20, which was reprinted in Deranty, Petherbridge, Rundell, and Sinnerbrink, *Recognition, Work, Politics*, 27–46.
51. Honneth's perspective differs from Charles Taylor's. See Charles Taylor, "The Politics of Recognition," in *Multiculturalism*, ed. Amy Gutmann (Princeton: Princeton University Press, 1994).
52. Cf. Honneth, *Freedom's Right*.
53. Jacques Rancière, *Hatred of Democracy*, trans. Steve Corcoran (New York: Verso, 2006).
54. The literature of Proust is analyzed by Rancière in *Mute Speech: Literature, Critical Theory, and Politics*, trans. by James Swenson (New York: Columbia University Press, 2011).
55. Honneth, *The Struggle for Recognition*, 171–180.
56. Axel Honneth, "On the Poverty of Our Liberty", text published in this volume.
57. Albert O. Hirschman, *Exit, Voice, and Loyalty: Responses to Decline in Firms, Organizations, and States* (Cambridge, Mass.: Harvard University Press, 1970).

### 2. BETWEEN HONNETH AND RANCIÈRE: PROBLEMS AND POTENTIALS OF A CONTEMPORARY CRITICAL THEORY OF SOCIETY

I would like to thank Alison Ross and Michael Olson for their many helpful stylistic suggestions.

1. See note 35 in Katia Genel's introduction, chapter 1 of this volume.
2. See Jacques Rancière, *Althusser's Lesson* (London: Continuum, 2011), 87.
3. Two seminal references that motivate this rejection of recognition in the "poststructuralist" paradigm are Lacan's pronouncement that subjective

formation is a process of "misrecognition" (*méconnaissance*) and Althusser's embrace and use of the Lacanian argument in his writings of the 1970s, particularly in "Ideology and Ideological State Apparatuses," in *Lenin and Philosophy, and Other Essays* (New York: Monthly Review Press, 1971), 161. Badiou's more recent dismissal of recognition (notably in Badiou, *Ethics: An Essay on the Understanding of Evil* [London: Verso, 2001], 20) can be read as a contemporary reappropriation of these two core references (indeed, see the reference to the mirror-stage at 21). As Alexander Garcia Düttman notes, however, one of the implications of Badiou's conception of politics as militant fidelity to an event might well be that it is in fact committed to conceiving of the latter in terms of a struggle for recognition, the struggle, namely, to have an egalitarian event and its practical implications acknowledged against its denial or foreclosure: see Düttman, "What Remains of Fidelity After Serious Thought," in *Think Again: Badiou and the Future of Philosophy*, ed. Peter Halward (London: Continuum, 2004), 206.

4. Alain Faure and Jacques Rancière, *La parole ouvrière* (Paris: La Fabrique Éditions, 2007), 7–19; Jacques Rancière, "Heretical Knowledge and the Emancipation of the Poor," in *Staging the People: The Proletarian and His Double* (London: Verso, 2011), 34–57.
5. Faure and Rancière, *La parole ouvrière*, 8.
6. Ibid., 9.
7. Rancière, "Heretical Knowledge and the Emancipation of the Poor."
8. Axel Honneth, "Domination and Moral Struggle," in *The Fragmented World of the Social* (New York: State University of New York Press, 1995), 3–14.
9. Faure and Rancière, *La parole ouvrière*, 12.
10. Ibid., 12.
11. Ibid., 9.
12. Jacques Rancière, *Disagreement: Politics and Philosophy*, trans. Julie Rose (Minneapolis: University of Minnesota Press, 1998), 53–55.
13. See p. 95 in this volume.
14. Jacques Rancière, "Le concept de critique et la critique de l'économie politique des 'Manuscrits de 1844' au 'Capital,'" in *Lire le Capital* (Paris: Presses Universitaires de France, 1996), 155.
15. See p. 90 in this volume.
16. Amy Allen, *The Politics of Ourselves* (New York: Columbia University Press, 2008) offers a compelling case for the central role a subject-concept can play across the different levels implied in a project in critical theory.

17. By "hermeneutic," therefore, I have in mind something different from what Christoph Menke highlighted in his intervention during the discussions in Frankfurt (see p. 108 in this volume). I am pointing not to a dimension of the political struggle itself, but rather to dimensions in Honneth's and Rancière's *methods*.
18. See, in particular, Axel Honneth, "Pathologies of the Social: The Past and Present of Social Philosophy," in *Disrespect: The Normative Foundations of Critical Theory* (Cambridge: Polity, 2007), 3–48.
19. See Heikki Ikäheimo, *Anerkennung* (Berlin: De Gruyter, 2014); and Ikäheimo, "Holism and Normative Essentialism in Hegel's Social Ontology," in *Recognition and Social Ontology*, ed. Heikki Ikäheimo and Arto Laitinen (Leiden: Brill, 2011), 145–209.
20. To refer only to Honneth's major books, chapter 6 of *The Struggle for Recognition*, which establishes a substantial link between everyday experiences of "disrespect" and the central role played by the notion in the theory of recognition, and chapter 3 of *Freedom's Right* are typical of this side of the hermeneutic moment. Axel Honneth, *The Struggle for Recognition: The Moral Grammar of Social Conflicts*, trans. Joel Anderson (Cambridge: Polity, 1994); Honneth, *Freedom's Right* (New York: Columbia University Press, 2014).
21. The second and third sections of chapter 5 of *The Struggle for Recognition* and the long normative reconstructions that make up the bulk of *Freedom's Right* are typical of this historical dimension of Honneth's hermeneutic methodology.
22. Recall that the three spheres of recognition were initially established as a "phenomenologically oriented typology": Honneth, *The Struggle for Recognition*, 93. This shift is palpable in particular in Honneth's adoption of Christopher Zurn's influential analysis of pathologies of recognition as "second-order" pathologies: see Christopher Zurn, "Social Pathologies as Second-Order Pathologies," in *Axel Honneth: Critical Essays*, ed. Danielle Petherbridge (Leiden: Brill Academic, 2011), 345–370.
23. See Emmanuel Renault, *L'expérience de l'injustice: Reconnaissance et clinique de l'injustice* (Paris: La Découverte, 2004); and Renault, *Souffrances sociales: Sociologie, psychologie, politique* (Paris: La Découverte, 2008); as well as Renault, "A Critical Theory of Social Suffering," *Critical Horizons* 11, no. 2 (2010): 221–241. See also Lois McNay, *The Misguided Search for the Political* (London: Polity, 2014), 28–65.
24. See Knox Peden, *Spinoza Contra Phenomenology: French Rationalism from Cavaillès to Deleuze* (Stanford: Stanford University Press, 2014).

25. Typical in this respect is the young Rancière's appeal to Lacanian theory and the friendly gesture toward Jacques-Alain Miller in his contribution to *Reading Capital*: see Louis Althusser, Roger Establet, Pierre Macherey, and Étienne Balibar, *Lire le Capital* (Paris: Presses Universitaires de France, 2008), 147, 185.
26. An interesting exception is constituted by the works of Deleuze and Guattari, whose decidedly anti-Lacanian materialism reaches well beyond structuralist strictures.
27. Alain Badiou, *Theory of the Subject* (London: Continuum, 2009); Badiou, *Being and Event* (London: Continuum, 2005), 431–440.
28. See Jacques Rancière, "Work, Identity, Subject," in *Jacques Rancière and the Contemporary Scene*, ed. J.-P. Deranty and A. Ross (London: Continuum, 2012), 205.
29. See Rancière, *Althusser's Lesson*, 21; Rancière, "Work, Identity, Subject," 207.
30. See Rancière, "Le concept de critique," 155: "The essential content of the subject-function is being mystified."
31. See, in particular, chapter 4 of *Althusser's Lesson*, "A Lesson in History," which already connects concrete reference to the historiography of the early labor movement with philosophical and political analysis. In this chapter, Rancière shows that the labor movement was waged in the name of the derided category of "the human being." The young Rancière concluded that this banished concept was in fact "the point that makes the very design of (Marxist) science possible." Rancière, *Althusser's Lesson*, 94.
32. Rancière, *Disagreement*, 7, 19, 55.
33. Jacques Rancière, *The Names of History: On the Poetics of Knowledge* (Minneapolis: University of Minnesota Press, 1992), 93.
34. Rancière, *Disagreement*, 47–55.
35. See Rainer Forst, *The Right to Justification* (New York: Columbia University Press, 2014), esp. 194–200. Forst's "critical model" of democracy (155–187)—which revolves around the gap immanent to society, between imperfect modes of justification and the critical potential inherent in "strict" justification that can always be acted upon to challenge the former—could be read in parallel with Rancière's conception of society as constituted around a torsion between factually existing hierarchies and their modes of self-assertion.
36. See, in particular, Honneth, "The Social Dynamics of Disrespect: On the Location of Critical Theory Today," in *Disrespect*, 63–79.

37. See the explicit account in Axel Honneth, "Work and Recognition: A Redefinition," in *The I in We: Studies in the Theory of Recognition* (Cambridge: Polity, 2012), 61–63.
38. Rancière, *Disagreement*, 43.
39. Rancière, *The Politics of Aesthetics* (London: Bloomsbury, 2006), 13.
40. See, especially, Étienne Balibar, *Equaliberty* (Durham: Duke University Press, 2014).
41. See, for instance, Amy Gutmann, *Liberal Equality* (Cambridge: Cambridge University Press, 1980).
42. See, for example, Kai Nielsen, *Equality and Liberty: A Defence of Radical Egalitarianism* (Totowa, N.J.: Rowman and Allanheld, 1985).
43. See, for example, Amartya Sen, *Inequality Reexamined* (Cambridge, Mass.: Harvard University Press, 1995), 21–23.
44. See Hannah Arendt, "The Perplexities of the Rights of Man," in *The Origins of Totalitarianism* (New York: Meridian, 1961), esp. 301; and Arendt, *The Human Condition* (Chicago: University of Chicago Press, 1958), 32; Bonnie Honig, *Antigone Interrupted* (Cambridge: Cambridge University Press, 2013); Linda Zerilli, *Feminism and the Abyss of Freedom* (Chicago: University of Chicago Press, 2005), which insists on the link between freedom and world-constitution among equals.
45. See Honneth, *The Struggle for Recognition*, 115–118; Honneth, "Redistribution as Recognition," in *Redistribution or Recognition: A Political-Philosophical Exchange*, by Nancy Fraser and Axel Honneth (London: Verso, 2003), 141–143.
46. Honneth, *Freedom's Right*, note 2, 337.
47. See Axel Honneth, "The Fabric of Justice: On the Limits of Contemporary Proceduralism," in *The I in We*, 35–55.
48. Honneth has noted the parallels between his approach and the perfectionist liberalism of Joseph Raz, as presented in Raz, *The Morality of Freedom* (Oxford: Clarendon, 1986). See Honneth, "Recognition and Justice: Outline of a Pluralist Theory of Justice," *Acta Sociologica* 47, no. 4 (2004): 351–364. There is not the space here to contrast Honneth's perfectionism and liberal perfectionism. It probably revolves around Honneth's strong emphasis on social relations as conditions of (perfectionist) autonomy. There would also be strong overlaps with Nussbaum's capacity approach, notably around the use of an anthropological mode of argumentation. In the article from 2004 just quoted, Honneth still talks about recognition as "quasi-transcendental interest of the human species."

49. Honneth, *Freedom's Right*, 43–50.
50. See Hauke Brunkhorst, *Solidarity: From Civic Friendship to a Global Legal Community* (Cambridge, Mass.: MIT Press, 2005), 55–78; Arto Laitinen and Birgitta Pessi, eds., *Solidarity: Theory and Practice* (Lanham, Md.: Lexington Books, 2014).
51. See the seminal critique in Iris Marion Young, *Justice and the Politics of Difference* (Princeton: Princeton University Press, 1990). See also Nancy Fraser's classical "Rethinking the Public Sphere: A Contribution to the Critique of Actually Existing Democracy," in *Justice Interruptus* (New York: Routledge, 1997), 69–98; and the first two chapters of Fraser, *Scales of Justice* (New York: Columbia University Press, 2010), 1–47.
52. Axel Honneth, "Philosophy as Social Research: David Miller's Theory of Justice," in *The I in We*, 119–134.
53. See Friedrich Engels, *Der Deutsche Bauernkrieg*, in *Karl Marx—Friedrich Engels—Werke* (Berlin: Dietz Verlag, 1960), 7:327–413; Peter Blickle, *Die Revolution von 1525* (Oldenburg: Oldenburg Wissenschaftsverlag, 2004).
54. See, for example, a recent interpretation of the Spartacus rebellion, which highlights the egalitarian ethos inspiring its leader, against the barbarity with which Roman civilization was treating its masses of slaves: Aldo Schiavone, *Spartacus* (Cambridge, Mass.: Harvard University Press, 2013), 52–61.
55. Jacques Rancière, "Politics, Identification and Subjectivisation," in *The Identity in Question*, ed. John Rajchman (New York: Routledge, 1995), 65.
56. As when Rancière defines politics as "the assumption of equality between any and every speaking being and by the concern to test this equality": Rancière, *Disagreement*, 30.
57. Jacques Rancière, *On the Shores of Politics*, trans. Liz Heron (London: Verso, 1995), 47–49.
58. See Rajchman, *The Identity in Question*.
59. See the ironic charge by the young Rancière that Althusser's theory of ideology is, in fact, a version of Durkheimian sociological thought: see Rancière, *Althusser's Lesson*, 131–132.
60. Alain Badiou, *Metapolitics*, trans. Jason Barker (New York: Verso, 2005), 98–99.
61. Ibid., 150. Indeed, the historical examples he uses are examples of collective organization and noninstitutional decision-making.
62. Badiou, *Being and Event*, 93–101.
63. Ibid., 95.

64. Rancière, *Althusser's Lesson*, 94.
65. Badiou, *Metapolitics*, 52–53, 98.
66. Ibid., 94.
67. Ibid.: "The task of philosophy is to expose politics to an assessment."
68. The famous passage in Engels and Marx is, of course, the incipit of the *Communist Manifesto*: "The history of all societies hitherto has been the history of class struggle."
69. Badiou, *L'hypothèse communiste* (Paris: Lignes, 2009), 190.
70. See, in particular, *L'hypothèse communiste*, in which the historical genealogy of egalitarian struggles is most consistently pursued, and the importance of "proper names" is established, notably at 196–198.
71. Indeed, Badiou directly refers to Rancière to contrast his emphasis on the "proper names" that incarnate revolutionary events with Rancière's focus on the anonymous heroes of revolutions (the Gauny's of history, we might say).
72. Rancière, *On the Shores of Politics*, 48.
73. Rancière, *The Names of History*, 93.
74. Jacques Rancière, *The Ignorant Schoolmaster: Five Lessons in Intellectual Emancipation*, trans. Kristin Ross (Stanford: Stanford University Press, 1991), 75–80.
75. See an explicit acknowledgment in Rancière, *La méthode de l'égalité* (Montrouge: Bayard, 2012), 90.
76. Jacques Rancière, *Film Fables*, trans. Emiliano Battista (Oxford: Berg, 2006).
77. Rancière, *Disagreement*, 37: "The modern political animal is first a literary animal."
78. See p. 102 in this volume.
79. However, this assumption is questioned in other fields, for instance, in the type of anthropological work that confronts its descriptive and normative results with the assumptions and conclusions of contemporary critical theory, for example and most eminently, Jack Goody: see, for example, Goody, *The Theft of History* (Cambridge: Cambridge University Press, 2006).
80. Axel Honneth, "A Communicative Disclosure of the Past: On the Relation Between Anthropology and Philosophy of History in Walter Benjamin," *New Formations* 20 (1993): 83–94. See Alison Ross, *Walter Benjamin's Concept of the Image* (New York: Routledge, 2014), chap. 4.
81. See Jessica Whyte, *Catastrophe and Redemption: The Political Thought of Giorgio Agamben* (New York: State University of New York Press, 2014).

82. James Tully, *Philosophy in a New Key* (Cambridge: Cambridge University Press, 2008); Tully, *On Global Citizenship: Dialogue with James Tully* (London: Bloomsbury Academic, 2014).
83. See, in particular, the chapter from 1999 "To Think and Act Differently: Foucault's Four Reciprocal Objections to Habermas' Critical Theory," in *Foucault Contra Habermas: Recasting the Dialogue Between Genealogy and Critical Theory*, ed. Samantha Avenshen and David Owen (London: Sage, 1999), 90–142.

## 3. CRITICAL QUESTIONS ON THE THEORY OF RECOGNITION

1. Jacques Rancière, *Disagreement: Politics and Philosophy*, trans. Julie Rose (Minneapolis: University of Minnesota Press, 1998), xii.

## 4. REMARKS ON THE PHILOSOPHICAL APPROACH OF JACQUES RANCIÈRE

This chapter was translated by Chad Kautzer, and the translation was modified by Jean-Philippe Deranty.

1. Axel Honneth, "Invisibility: On the Epistemology of 'Recognition,'" *Aristotelian Society*, supplementary volume 75 (2001): 111–126.
2. For a similar type of approach, see Axel Honneth, "Moral Consciousness and Class Domination: Some Problems in the Analysis of Hidden Morality," in *Disrespect: The Normative Foundations of Critical Theory* (Cambridge: Polity, 2007), 80–96; and Honneth, "Anerkennungsbeziehungen und Moral: Eine Diskussionsbemerkung zur Anthropologischen Erweiterung der Diskursethik," in *Anthropologie, Ethik und Gesellschaft: Für Helmut Fahrenbach*, ed. R. Brunner and P. Kelbel (Frankfurt: Campus Verlag, 2000), 101–111.

## 5. A CRITICAL DISCUSSION

1. Jacques Rancière refers to Jeanne Désirée Deroin (1805–1894), a French socialist feminist; see Jacques Rancière, *Proletarian Nights. The Workers' Dream in Nineteenth Century France*, trans. J. Drury (London: Verso, 2014), 108–110, and especially the epilogue; see also Rancière, *Disagreement: Politics and Philosophy*, trans. Julie Rose (Minneapolis: University of Minnesota Press, 1998), 41.

2. Pierre Bourdieu, *La misère du monde* (Paris: Le Seuil, 1993); English version: Bourdieu, *Weight of the World: Social Suffering in Contemporary Society* (Cambridge: Polity, 1999).

## 6. THE METHOD OF EQUALITY: POLITICS AND POETICS

1. "Le travail à la tâche," in Jacques Rancière, *Proletarian Nights: The Workers' Dream in Nineteenth-Century France*, trans. John Drury (London: Verso, 2012), 81.

## 7. OF THE POVERTY OF OUR LIBERTY: THE GREATNESS AND LIMITS OF HEGEL'S DOCTRINE OF ETHICAL LIFE

This chapter was translated by Felix Koch and revised by Jean-Philippe Deranty.

1. Isaiah Berlin, "Two Concepts of Liberty," in *Four Essays on Liberty* (Oxford: Oxford University Press, 1990). Critical remarks and suggestions for further distinctions are found in Raymond Geuss, "Auffassungen der Freiheit," *Zeitschrift für philosophische Forschung* 49 (1995): 1–14; and Axel Honneth, *Freedom's Right: The Social Foundations of Democratic Life*, trans. Joseph Ganahl (New York: Columbia University Press, 2014), section A.
2. Dieter Henrich, "Zerfall und Zukunft: Hegels Theoreme über das Ende der Kunst," in *Fixpunkte: Abhandlungen und Essays zur Theorie der Kunst* (Frankfurt: Suhrkamp, 2003), 65–125, esp. 65.
3. On this conception of reason, see Dina Emundts and Rolf-Peter Horstmann, *G. W. F. Hegel: Eine Einführung* (Stuttgart: Philipp Reclam, 2002), 69–75.
4. I am alluding to the social ontology of John Searle, which bears some surprising but as yet unexplored similarities with Hegel's theory of objective spirit. See John R. Searle, *The Construction of Social Reality* (New York: Free Press, 1995), esp. chap. 2.
5. On the historical presuppositions of Hegel's own philosophy of right, see the famous passage in his preface stating that reason has attained actuality only in the present, G. W. F. Hegel, *Elements of the Philosophy of Right* (Cambridge: Cambridge University Press, 1991), 19.
6. G. W. F. Hegel, *Lectures on the Philosophy of World History*, trans. H. B. Nisbet (Cambridge: Cambridge University Press, 1984).

7. On this process of a successive extrication of spirit (conceived as subject) from "natural necessity," see Hegel, *Philosophy of World History*, 44–123. See also G. W. F. Hegel, *Philosophy of Mind*, trans. M. Inwood (Oxford: Oxford University Press, 2010), §552, 229. Concerning the method of Hegel's philosophy of history, which is here described as "genealogical," see Christoph Menke, "Geist und Leben: Zu einer genealogischen Kritik der Phänomenologie," in *Von der Logik zur Sprache: Stuttgarter Hegel-Kongress 2005*, ed. R. Bubner and G. Hindrichs (Stuttgart: Klett-Cotta, 2005), 321–348.
8. Hegel, *Philosophy of Right*, §4, pp. 35–37.
9. Ibid., §§11–32, pp. 45–62.
10. Ibid., §11–13, pp. 45–46.
11. Ibid., §44.
12. Ibid., §14, pp. 47–48.
13. Ibid., §15, Addition: "It is inherent in arbitrariness that the content is not determined as mine by the nature of my will, but by contingency; thus I am also dependent on this content, and this is the contradiction which underlies arbitrariness."
14. See Hegel, *Philosophy of Mind*, §484, p. 217: "But the purposive action of this will is to realize its concept, freedom, in the externally objective realm, making it a world determined by the will, so that in it the will is at home with itself, joined together with itself: the concept accordingly completed to the Idea."
15. For this reason, volume 3 of Hegel's *Encyclopedia* introduces the concept of "custom" (as "habit, temper, and character") directly after the first mention of "objective" freedom, that is, freedom that has been "shaped into the actuality of a world" (§484): for its "authoritative power" to exist, it needs to be "impressed in the subjective will, not in the form of feeling and urge, but in its universality, . . . as disposition and character, and is the will's custom." Hegel, *Philosophy of Mind*, §485, p. 218.
16. Hegel, *Philosophy of Right*, §7, Addition, pp. 41–42.
17. See my own attempt at explicating this idea: Axel Honneth, *Freedom's Right*, section A, III, esp. pp. 82–87. Despite some disagreements, my work is indebted to Frederick Neuhouser, *Foundations of Hegel's Social Theory: Actualizing Freedom* (Cambridge, Mass.: Harvard University Press, 2000), esp. chap. 1.
18. On this expansion of the concept of right in Hegel, see Ludwig Siep, "Philosophische Begründung des Rechts bei Fichte und Hegel," in *Praktische Philosophie im Deutschen Idealismus* (Frankfurt: Suhrkamp, 1992), 65–80.

19. Hegel, *Philosophy of Right*, §20, p. 52.
20. On the socializing function of ethical life, see Robert B. Pippin, *Hegel's Practical Philosophy: Rational Agency as Ethical Life* (Cambridge: Cambridge University Press, 2008), esp. part 3. Hegel himself offers a vivid description of the processes by which modern subjects are socialized in his lectures on aesthetics, when he discusses the historical and social preconditions of romantic art. G. W. F. Hegel, *Aesthetics: Lectures on Fine Art* (Oxford: Clarendon, 1988), esp. 517–519.
21. This becomes especially clear in Émile Durkheim's distinction between morals of the family, professional ethics, and civic morals in Durkheim, *Professional Ethics and Civic Morals* (London: Routledge, 1992).
22. See Hegel's sober summary in *Philosophy of Right*, §157, pp. 197–198. Of course, this list and also the subsequent characterizations of the three ethical spheres are no longer indicative of the great efforts of sociological condensation and conceptual abstraction that were required to carve out the specificity of social freedom. On the analysis of the market economy alone, see Birger P. Priddat, *Hegel als Ökonom* (Berlin: Duncker und Humblot, 1990).
23. Hegel, *Philosophy of Right*, §165, p. 206; Hegel, *Philosophy of Mind*, §518, p. 229.
24. Hegel, *Philosophy of Right*, §182, §187, p. 220, p. 224.
25. Ibid., §264 and §268 on patriotism, p. 287, p. 289.
26. See, among others, Susanne Brauer, *Natur und Sittlichkeit: Die Familie in Hegels Rechtsphilosophie* (Freiburg: Karl Alber Verlag, 2007).
27. Michael Theunissen. "The Repressed Intersubjectivity in Hegel's Philosophy of Right," in *Hegel and Legal Theory*, ed. Drucilla Cornell, Michel Rosenfeld, and David Carlson (New York: Routledge, 1991), 3–63.
28. Hegel, *Philosophy of Right*, §§34–104, pp. 67–131.
29. Ibid., §§105–141, pp. 135–186.
30. A. O. Hirschman, *Exit, Voice, and Loyalty: Responses to Decline in Firms, Organizations, and States* (Cambridge, Mass.: Harvard University Press, 1970).
31. See the transcript of Hegel's 1819–1820 lecture on the philosophy of right: G. W. F. Hegel, *Philosophie des Rechts: Die Vorlesung von 1819/20 in einer Nachschrift* (Frankfurt: Suhrkamp, 1983), esp. 187–207. The section on civil society makes repeated reference to the "outrage" that the poor must justifiably feel in view of their situation. In this context Hegel also speaks of an "emergency right" to political revolt.

# BIBLIOGRAPHY

## HONNETH

### WORKS BY AXEL HONNETH

#### Monographs, Collections of Essays, and Edited Collections

The years in this list indicate the date of the original publication, though the translations (with a later publication date) are cited.


1980

Honneth, Axel, and Hans Jonas. *Social Action and Human Nature.* Translated by Raymond Meyer. Cambridge: Cambridge University Press, 1988.

1985

Honneth, Axel. *Critique of Power: Reflective Stages in a Critical Social Theory.* Translated by Kenneth Baynes. Cambridge, Mass.: MIT Press, 1991.

1989

Honneth, Axel, Thomas McCarthy, Claus Offe, and Albrecht Wellmer. *Cultural-Political Interventions in the Unfinished Project of Enlightenment.* Translated by Barbara Fultner. Cambridge, Mass.: MIT Press, 1992.

——. *Philosophical Interventions in the Unfinished Project of Enlightenment.* Translated by William Rehg. Cambridge, Mass.: MIT Press, 1992.

1990

Honneth, Axel. *The Fragmented World of the Social: Essays in Social and Political Philosophy.* Edited by Charles W. Wright. Albany: State University of New York Press, 1995.

1992

Honneth, Axel. *The Struggle for Recognition: The Moral Grammar of Social Conflicts.* Translated by Joel Anderson. Cambridge: Polity, 1994.

1994

Honneth, Axel. *Desintegration: Bruchstücke einer soziologischen Zeitdiagnose.* Frankfurt: Fischer, 1994.

1999

Honneth, Axel. *Suffering from Indeterminacy: An Attempt at a Reactualization of Hegel's Philosophy of Right: Two Lectures.* Spinoza Lectures. Amsterdam: Uitgeverij Van Gorcum, 2000.

2000

Honneth, Axel. *Disrespect: The Normative Foundations of Critical Theory.* Translated by Joseph Ganahl. Cambridge: Polity, 2007.

2001

Honneth, Axel. *The Pathologies of Individual Freedom: Hegel's Social Theory.* Translated by Ladislaus Löb. Princeton: Princeton University Press, 2010.

2003

Fraser, Nancy, and Axel Honneth. *Redistribution or Recognition? A Political-Philosophical Exchange.* Translated by Joel Golb, James Ingram, and Christiane Wilke. London: Verso, 2003.

2005

Honneth, Axel. *Reification: A New Look at an Old Idea.* Edited by Martin Jay. Oxford: Oxford University Press, 2008.

2007

Honneth, Axel. *Pathologies of Reason: On the Legacy of Critical Theory.* Translated by James Ingram. New York: Columbia University Press, 2009.

2010

Honneth, Axel. *The I in We: Studies in the Theory of Recognition.* Translated by Joseph Ganahl. Cambridge: Polity, 2012.

2011

Honneth, Axel. *Freedom's Right: The Social Foundations of Democratic Life.* Translated by Joseph Ganahl. New York: Columbia University Press, 2014.

2014

Honneth, Axel. *Vivisektionen eines Zeitalters: Porträts zur Ideengeschichte des 20. Jahrhunderts.* Frankfurt: Suhrkamp, 2014.

2015

Honneth, Axel. *Die Idee des Sozialismus: Versuch einer Aktualisierung.* Frankfurt: Suhrkamp, 2015.

## Journal Articles and Book Chapters



Honneth, Axel. "Atomism and Ethical Life: on Hegel's Critique of the French Revolution." In *Universalism Versus Communitarianism*, edited by D. Rasmussen, 129–138. Cambridge, Mass.: MIT Press, 1989.

——. "Between Hermeneutics and Hegelianism: John McDowell and the Challenge of Moral Realism." In *Reading McDowell, On Mind and World*, edited by Nicholas Smith, 246–265. London: Routledge, 2002.

——. "Between Proceduralism and Teleology: An Unresolved Conflict in Dewey's Moral Theory." *Transactions of the Charles S. Peirce Society* 34, no. 3 (1998): 689–711.

——. "Brutalization of the Social Conflict: Struggles for Recognition in the Early 21st Century." *Distinktion: Scandinavian Journal of Social Theory* 13, no. 1 (2012): 5–19.

——. "Considerations on Alessandro Ferrara's Reflective Authenticity." *Philosophy and Social Criticism* 30, no. 1 (2004): 11–16.

——. "Grounding Recognition: A Rejoinder to Critical Questions." *Inquiry* 45, no. 4 (2002): 499–519.

——. "Herbert Marcuse and the Frankfurt School." *Radical Philosophy Review* 16, no. 1 (2013): 49–57.

——. "History and Interaction." In *Althusser: A Critical Reader*, edited by Gregory Elliott, 73–91. Oxford: Blackwell, 1994.

——. "Integrity and Disrespect: Principles of a Conception of Morality Based on the Theory of Recognition." *Political Theory* 20, no. 2 (1992): 187–201.

——. "Invisibility: On the Epistemology of 'Recognition.'" *Aristotelian Society*, supplementary volume 65: 111–126.

——. "Justice as Institutionalized Freedom: A Hegelian Perspective." In *Dialectics, Self-Consciousness, and Recognition: The Hegelian Legacy*, edited by Asger Sørensen, Morten Raffnsøe-Møller, and Arne Grøn. Uppsala: NSU Press, 2009.

——. "Liberty's Entanglements: Bob Dylan and His Era." *Philosophy and Social Criticism* 36, no. 7 (2010): 777–783.

——. "Literary Imagination and Morality: A Modest Query of an Immodest Proposal." *Philosophy and Social Criticism* 24, nos. 2–3 (1998): 41–47.

——. "Max Horkheimer and the Sociological Deficit of Critical Theory." In *On Horkheimer*, edited by Seyla Benhabib, Wolfgang Bonß, and John McCole, 187–214. Cambridge, Mass.: MIT Press, 1993.

——. "Michael Walzer, Interpretation and Social Criticism." *Thesis Eleven* 36 (1993): 188–194.

——. "Moral Development and Social Struggle: Hegel's Early Social-Philosophical Doctrines." In *Cultural-Political Interventions in the Unfinished Project of Enlightenment*, by Axel Honneth, Thomas McCarthy, Claus Offe, and Albrecht Wellmer, translated by Barbara Fultner, 197–218. Cambridge, Mass.: MIT Press, 1992.

——. "The Normativity of Ethical Life." *Philosophy and Social Criticism* 40, no. 8 (2014): 817–826.

——. "On the Destructive Power of the Third: Gadamer and Heidegger's Theory of Intersubjectivity." *Philosophy and Social Criticism* 29, no. 1 (2003): 5–21.

——. "Pluralization and Recognition: On the Self-Mis-Understanding of Postmodern Social Theorists." In *Between Totalitarianism and Postmodernity: A Thesis Eleven Reader*, edited by Peter Beilharz, Gillian Robinson, and John Rundell, 163–173. Cambridge, Mass.: MIT Press, 1992.

——. "The Political Identity of the Green Movement in Germany: Social-Philosophical Reflections." *Critical Horizons* 11, no. 1 (2010): 5–18.

——. "Postmodern Identity and Object-Relations Theory: On the Seeming Obsolescence of Psychoanalysis." *Philosophical Explorations* 2, no. 3 (1999): 225–242.

——. "Problems of Ethical Pluralism: Arnold Gehlen's Anthropological Ethics." *Iris* 1, no. 1 (2009): 187–194.

——. "Recognition and Justice: Outline of a Plural Theory of Justice." *Acta Sociologica* 47 (2004): 351–364.

——. "Recognition and Moral Obligation." *Social Research* 64, no. 1 (1997): 16–35.

——. "Recognition as Ideology." In *Recognition and Power: Axel Honneth and the Tradition of Critical Social Theory*, edited by Bert van den Brink and David Owen, 323–348. New York: Cambridge University Press, 2007.

——. "Recognition or Redistribution? Changing Perspectives on the Moral Order of Society." *Theory, Culture and Society* 18, nos. 2–3 (2001): 43–55.

——. "Rejoinder." *Critical Horizons* 16, no. 2 (2015): 204–226.

——. "Replies." *Krisis* 1 (2013): 37–47.

——. "Reply to Andreas Kalyvas, *Critical Theory at the Crossroads: Comments on Axel Honneth's Theory of Recognition*." *European Journal of Social Theory* 2, no. 2 (1999): 249–252.

——. "A Society Without Humiliation? On Avishai Margalit's Draft of a 'Decent Society.'" *Journal of Philosophy* 5, no. 3 (1997): 306–324.

Honneth, Axel, and Joel Anderson. "Autonomy, Vulnerability, Recognition, and Justice." In *Autonomy and the Challenges to Liberalism: New Essays*, edited by John Christman and Joel Anderson, 77–100. New York: Cambridge University Press, 2005.

Honneth, Axel, Peter Osborne, and Stale Finke. "Critical Theory in Germany Today: An Interview with Alex Honneth." *Radical Philosophy: A Journal of Socialist and Feminist Philosophy* 65 (1993): 33–40.

Honneth, Axel, A. Petersen, and R. Willig. "An Interview with Axel Honneth." *European Journal of Philosophy* 5, no. 2 (2002): 265–277.

## STUDIES ON AXEL HONNETH AND HONNETH'S RECOGNITION THEORY

### Books

Bankovsky, Miriam. *Perfecting Justice in Rawls, Habermas and Honneth: A Deconstructive Perspective*. London: Bloomsbury, 2014.

Bankovsky, Miriam, and Alice Le Goff, eds. *Recognition Theory and Contemporary French Moral and Political Philosophy: Reopening the Dialogue*. Manchester: Manchester University Press, 2012.

Brink, Bert van den, and David Owen. *Recognition and Power: Axel Honneth and the Tradition of Critical Social Theory*. Cambridge: Cambridge University Press, 2007.

Caillé, Alain, ed. *De la reconnaissance: Don, identité et estime de soi*. Paris: La Découverte, 2004.

Deranty, Jean-Philippe. *Beyond Communication: A Critical Study of Axel Honneth's Social Philosophy*. Leiden: Brill, 2009.

Deranty, Jean-Philippe, Danielle Petherbridge, John Rundell, and Robert Sinnerbrink, eds. *Recognition, Work, Politics: New Directions in French Critical Theory*. Leiden: Brill, 2007.

Huttunen, Rauno. *Habermas, Honneth and Education*. Cologne: Lambert Academic, 2009.

Iser, Matthias. *Empörung und Fortschritt: Grundlagen einer Kritischen Theorie der Gesellschaft*. Frankfurt: Campus, 2008.

Jakobsen, Jonas, and Odin Lysaker, eds. *Recognition and Freedom: Axel Honneth's Political Thought*. Leiden: Brill, 2015.

Lazzeri, Christian, and Soraya Nour, eds. *Reconnaissance, identité et intégration sociale*. Nanterre: Presses Universitaires de Paris Ouest, 2009.

Maia, Rousiley. *Recognition and the Media*. London: Palgrave Macmillan, 2014.

McNay, Lois. *Against Recognition*. London: Polity, 2007.

O'Neill, Shane, and Nicholas Smith. *Recognition Theory as Social Research: Investigating the Dynamics of Social Conflict*. London: Palgrave Macmillan, 2012.

Petherbridge, Danielle, ed. *Axel Honneth: Critical Essays, with a Reply by Axel Honneth*. Leiden: Brill, 2011.

——. *The Critical Theory of Axel Honneth*. Lanham, Md.: Lexington, 2013.

Renault, Emmanuel, and Yves Sintomer, eds. *Où en est la théorie critique?* Paris: La Découverte, 2003.

Schmidt-am-Busch, Hans-Christoph, and Christopher Zurn, eds. *The Philosophy of Recognition: Historical and Contemporary Perspectives*. Lanham, Md.: Lexington Books, 2009.

Thompson, Simon. *The Political Theory of Recognition: A Critical Introduction*. Cambridge: Polity, 2006.

Zurn, Christopher. *Axel Honneth*. Cambridge: Polity, 2015.

## Journal Articles

Alexander, Jeffrey, and Maria Pia Lara. "Honneth's New Critical Theory of Recognition." *New Left Review* 220 (1996): 126–152.

Allen, Jonathan. "Decency and the Struggle for Recognition." *Social Theory and Practice* 24 (1998): 449–469.

Anderson, Joel. "The Fragile Accomplishment of Social Freedom." *Krisis* 1 (2013): 18–22.

Bankovsky, Miriam. "Social Justice: Defending Rawls' Theory of Justice Against Honneth's Objections." *Philosophy and Social Criticism* 36, no. 1 (2009): 95–118.

Bedorf, Thomas. "Zu Zweit oder zu Dritt? Intersubjektivität, Anti-Sozialität und die Whitebook-Honneth Kontroverse." *Psyche* 58 (2004): 1–19.

Bernstein, Jay. "Suffering Injustice: Misrecognition as Moral Injury in Critical Theory." *International Journal of Philosophical Studies* 13, no. 3 (2005): 303–324.

Boer, Karin de. "Beyond Recognition? Critical Reflections on Honneth's Reading of Hegel's Philosophy of Right." *International Journal of Philosophical Studies* 21, no. 4 (2013): 534–558.

Bohman, James. "Beyond Distributive Justice and Struggles for Recognition: Freedom, Democracy, and Critical Theory." *European Journal of Political Theory* 6, no. 3 (2007): 267–276.

Borman, David A. "Labour, Exchange and Recognition: Marx Contra Honneth." *Philosophy and Social Criticism* 35, no. 8 (2009): 935–959.

Brink, Bert van den. "From Personal Relations to the Rest of Society." *Krisis* 1 (2013): 23–27.

Chari, Anita. "Toward a Political Critique of Reification: Lukacs, Honneth and the Aims of Critical Theory." *Philosophy and Social Criticism* 36, no. 5 (2010): 587–606.

Claassen, Rutger. "Social Freedom and the Demands of Justice: A Study of Honneth's *Recht Der Freiheit.*" *Constellations* 21, no. 1 (2014): 67–82.

Deranty, Jean-Philippe. "Injustice, Violence and Social Struggle: The Critical Potential of Axel Honneth's Theory of Recognition." *Critical Horizons* 5, no. 1 (2004): 297–322.

——. "The Loss of Nature in Axel Honneth's Social Philosophy: Rereading Mead with Merleau-Ponty." *Critical Horizons* 6, no. 1 (2005): 153–181.

——. "Marx, Honneth and the Tasks of a Contemporary Critical Theory." *Ethical Theory and Moral Practice* 16, no. 4 (2013): 745–758.

——. "Repressed Materiality: Retrieving the Materialism in Axel Honneth's Theory of Recognition." *Critical Horizons* 7, no. 1 (2006): 113–140.

Deranty, Jean-Philippe, and Emmanuel Renault. "Politicising Honneth's Ethics of Recognition." *Thesis Eleven* 88 (2007): 92–111.

Ferrara, Alessandro. "The Relation of Authenticity to Normativity: A Response to Larmore and Honneth." *Philosophy and Social Criticism* 30, no. 1 (2004): 17–24.

Forst, Rainer. "First Things First Redistribution, Recognition and Justification." *European Journal of Political Theory* 6, no. 3 (2007): 291–304.

Foster, Roger. "An Adornian Theory of Recognition? A Critical Response to Axel Honneth's Reification: A New Look at an Old Idea." *International Journal of Philosophical Studies* 19, no. 2 (2011): 255–265.

——. "Recognition and Resistance: Axel Honneth's Critical Social Theory." *Radical Philosophy* 94 (1999): 6–18.

Freyenhagen, Fabian. "Honneth on Social Pathologies: A Critique." *Critical Horizons* 16, no. 2 (2015): 131–152.

Gabriels, René. "There Must Be Some Way Out of Here: In Search of a Critical Theory of World Society." *Krisis* 1 (2013): 5–9.

Hedrick, Todd. "Reification in and Through Law: Elements of a Theory in Marx, Lukacs, and Honneth." *European Journal of Political Theory* 13, no. 2 (2014): 178–198.

Heidegren, Carl-Göran. "Anthropology, Social Theory, and Politics: Axel Honneth's Theory of Recognition." *Inquiry* 45, no. 4 (2002): 433–446.

Heins, Volker. "Of Persons and Peoples: Internationalizing the Critical Theory of Recognition." *Contemporary Political Theory* 9, no. 2 (2010): 149–170.

——. "The Place of Property in the Politics of Recognition." *Constellations* 16, no. 4 (2009): 579–592.

——. "Realizing Honneth: Redistribution, Recognition, and Global Justice." *Journal of Global Ethics* 4, no. 2 (2008): 141–153.

——. “Three Meanings of Equality: The ‘Arab Problem’ in Israel.” *Res Publica* 18, no. 1 (2012): 79–91.

Held, Jacob. “Axel Honneth and the Future of Critical Theory.” *Radical Philosophy Review* 11, no. 2 (2008): 175–186.

Huttunen, Rauno, and Mark Murphy. “Discourse and Recognition as Normative Grounds for Radical Pedagogy: Habermasian and Honnethian Ethics in the Context of Education.” *Studies in Philosophy and Education* 31, no. 2 (2012): 137–152.

Ikäheimo, Heikki. “On the Genus and Species of Recognition.” *Inquiry* 45, no. 4 (2002): 447–462.

——. “A Vital Human Need Recognition as Inclusion in Personhood.” *European Journal of Political Theory* 8, no. 1 (2009): 31–45.

Jansen, Yolande. “The ‘Us’ of Democratic Will-Formation and Globalisation.” *Krisis* 1 (2013): 32–36.

Jütten, Timo. “Is the Market a Sphere of Social Freedom?” *Critical Horizons* 16, no. 2 (2015): 187–203.

——. “What Is Reification? A Critique of Axel Honneth.” *Inquiry* 53, no. 3 (2010): 235–256.

Kalyvas, Andreas. “Critical Theory at the Crossroads: Comments on Axel Honneth’s Theory of Recognition.” *European Journal of Social Theory* 2, no. 1 (1999): 99–108.

Kautzer, Chad. “Self-Defensive Subjectivity: The Diagnosis of a Social Pathology.” *Philosophy and Social Criticism* 40, no. 8 (2014): 743–756.

Kompridis, Nikolas. “From Reason to Self-Realisation? Axel Honneth and the ‘Ethical Turn’ in Critical Theory.” *Critical Horizons* 5, no. 1 (2004): 323–360.

——. “On the Task of Social Philosophy: A Reply to Axel Honneth.” *Social Philosophy Today* 17 (2003): 235–251.

——. “Struggling Over the Meaning of Recognition: A Matter of Identity, Justice, or Freedom?” *European Journal of Political Theory* 6, no. 3 (2007): 277–289.

Laitinen, Arto. “Interpersonal Recognition: A Response to Value or a Precondition of Personhood.” *Inquiry* 45, no. 4 (2002): 463–478.

——. “Recognition, Needs and Wrongness: Two Approaches.” *European Journal of Political Theory* 8, no. 1 (2009): 13–30.

Leeuwen, Bart van. “A Formal Recognition of Social Attachments: Expanding Axel Honneth’s Theory of Recognition.” *Inquiry* 50, no. 2 (2007): 180–205.

Mark, D. Clifton. “Recognition and Honor: A Critique of Axel Honneth’s and Charles Taylor’s Histories of Recognition.” *Constellations* 21, no. 1 (2014): 16–31.

McBride, Cillian. "Deliberative Democracy and the Politics of Recognition." *Political Studies* 53 (2005): 497–515.

McNay, Lois. "Social Freedom and Progress in the Family: Reflections on Care, Gender and Inequality." *Critical Horizons* 16, no. 2 (2015): 170–186.

——. "The Trouble with Recognition: Subjectivity, Suffering, and Agency." *Sociological Theory* 26, no. 3 (2008): 271–296.

McNeil, David. "Social Freedom and Self-Actualization: 'Normative Reconstruction' as a Theory of Justice." *Critical Horizons* 16, no. 2 (2015): 153–169.

McQueen, Paddy. "Honneth, Butler and the Ambivalent Effects of Recognition." *Res Publica* 21, no. 1 (2015): 43–60.

Moyaert, Marianne. "Between Ideology and Utopia: Honneth and Ricoeur on Symbolic Violence, Marginalization and Recognition." *Ricoeur Studies* 2, no. 1 (2011): 84–109.

Nys, Thomas. "Which Justice, Whose Pathology." *Krisis* 1 (2013): 10–13.

Pilapil, Renante D. "Disrespect and Political Resistance Honneth and the Theory of Recognition." *Thesis Eleven* 114 (2013): 48–60.

——. "From Psychologism to Personhood: Honneth, Recognition, and the Making of Persons." *Res Publica* 18, no. 1 (2012): 39–51.

Pippin, Robert. "Reconstructivism: On Honneth's Hegelianism." *Philosophy and Social Criticism* 40, no. 8 (2014): 725–741.

Presbey, Gail M. "The Struggle for Recognition in the Philosophy of Axel Honneth, Applied to the Current South African Situation and its Call for an 'African Renaissance.'" *Philosophy and Social Criticism* 29, no. 5 (2003): 537–561.

Renault, Emmanuel. "Three Marxian Approaches to Recognition." *Ethical Theory and Moral Practice* 16, no. 4 (2013): 699–711.

Rocheleau, Jordy. "Communication, Recognition and Politics: Reconciling the Critical Theories of Honneth and Habermas." *Social Philosophy Today* 17 (2003): 253–263.

Rogers, Melvin R. "Rereading Honneth: Exodus Politics and the Paradox of Recognition." *European Journal of Political Theory* 8, no. 2 (2009): 183–206.

Rössler, Beate. "Kantian Autonomy and Its Social Preconditions: On Axel Honneth's Das Recht der Freiheit." *Krisis* 1 (2013): 14–17.

Schaap, Andrew. "Political Reconciliation Through a Struggle for Recognition?" *Social and Legal Studies* 13, no. 4 (2004): 523–540.

Schaub, Jörg. "Misdevelopments, Pathologies, and Normative Revolutions: Normative Reconstruction as Method of Critical Theory." *Critical Horizons* 16, no. 2 (2015): 107–130.

Schweiger, Gottfried. "Recognition Theory and Global Poverty." *Journal of Global Ethics* 10, no. 3 (2014): 267–273.

Seglow, Jonathan. "Rights, Contribution, Achievement and the World Some Thoughts on Honneth's Recognitive Ideal." *European Journal of Political Theory* 8, no. 1 (2009): 61–75.

Smith, Nicholas H. "Work and the Struggle for Recognition." *European Journal of Political Theory* 8, no. 1 (2009): 46–60.

Smith, Nicholas H., and Jean-Philippe Deranty. "Work and the Politics of Misrecognition." *Res Publica* 18, no. 1 (2012): 53–64.

Staples, Kelly. "Statelessness and the Politics of Misrecognition." *Res Publica* 18, no. 1 (2012): 93–106.

Strydom, Piet. "Cognition and Recognition: On the Problem of the Cognitive in Honneth." *Philosophy and Social Criticism* 38, no. 6 (2012): 591–607.

Thompson, Michael J. "Axel Honneth and the Neo-Idealist Turn in Critical Theory." *Philosophy and Social Criticism* 40, no. 8 (2014): 779–797.

Thompson, Simon. "Is Redistribution a Form of Recognition? Comments on the Fraser-Honneth Debate." *Critical Review of International Social and Political Philosophy* 8, no. 1 (2006): 85–102.

Tully, James. "Struggles Over Recognition and Distribution." *Constellations* 7, no. 4 (2000): 469–482.

Varga, Somogy. "Critical Theory and the Two-Level Account of Recognition—Towards a New Foundation?" *Critical Horizons* 11, no. 1 (2010): 19–33.

Yar, Majid. "Honneth and the Communitarians: Towards a Recognitive Critical Theory of Community." *Res Publica* 9 (2003): 101–125.

Zurn, Christopher. "Anthropology and Normativity: A Critique of Axel Honneth's 'Formal Conceptions of Ethical Life.'" *Philosophy and Social Criticism* 26, no. 1 (2000): 115–124.

——. "Identity or Status? Struggles over 'Recognition' in Fraser, Honneth, and Taylor." *Constellations* 10, no. 4 (2003): 519–537.

——. "Recognition, Redistribution, and Democracy: Dilemmas of Honneth's Critical Social Theory." *European Journal of Philosophy* 13, no. 1 (2005): 89–126.

# RANCIÈRE

## WORKS BY JACQUES RANCIÈRE

### Monographs, Collections of Essays, and Edited Collections

The years in this list indicate the date of the original publication, though the translations (with a later publication date) are cited.

1974

Rancière, Jacques. *Althusser's Lesson*. Translated by Emiliano Battista. London: Continuum, 2011.

1976

Rancière Jacques, with Alain Faure. *La parole ouvrière*. Paris: 10/18, 1976. Reprinted in Paris by La Fabrique in 2007.

1981

Rancière, Jacques. *Proletarian Nights: The Workers' Dream in Nineteenth-Century France*. Translated by John Drury. London: Verso, 2012.

1983

Rancière, Jacques. *The Philosopher and His Poor*. Translated by John Drury, Corinne Oyster, and Andrew Parker. Durham: Duke University Press, 2004.

1987

Rancière, Jacques. *The Ignorant Schoolmaster: Five Lessons in Intellectual Emancipation*. Translated by Kristin Ross. Stanford: Stanford University Press, 1991.

1990

Rancière, Jacques. *Short Voyages to the Land of the People*. Translated by James B. Swenson. Stanford: Stanford University Press, 2003.

1992

Rancière, Jacques. *The Names of History: On the Poetics of Knowledge*. Translated by Hassan Melehy. Minneapolis: University of Minnesota Press, 1994.

——. *On the Shores of Politics*. Translated by Liz Heron. London: Verso, 1995. Revised in 1998.

1995

Rancière, Jacques. *Disagreement: Politics and Philosophy*. Translated by Julie Rose. Minneapolis: University of Minnesota Press, 1998.

1996

Rancière, Jacques. *Mallarmé: The Politics of the Siren*. Translated by Steve Corcoran. London: Continuum, 2011.

1998

Rancière, Jacques. *The Flesh of Words: The Politics of Writing.* Translated by Charlotte Mandel. Stanford: Stanford University Press, 2004.

——. *Mute Speech: Literature, Critical Theory, and Politics.* Introduction by Gabriel Rockhill. Translated by James Swenson. New York: Columbia University Press, 2011.

2000

Rancière, Jacques. *The Politics of Aesthetics: The Distribution of the Sensible.* Translated by Gabriel Rockhill. London: Continuum, 2004.

2001

Rancière, Jacques. *The Aesthetic Unconscious.* Translated by Debra Keates and James Swenson. Cambridge: Polity, 2009.

——. *Film Fables.* Translated by Emiliano Battista. Oxford: Berg, 2006.

2003

Rancière, Jacques. *The Future of the Image.* Translated by Gregory Elliot. New York: Verso, 2007.

——. *Staging the People: The Proletarian and His Double.* Translated by David Fernbach. London: Verso, 2011.

——. *Staging the People.* Vol. 2, *The Intellectual and His People.* Translated by David Fernbach. London: Verso, 2012.

2004

Rancière, Jacques. *Aesthetics and Its Discontents.* Translated by Steve Corcoran. Cambridge: Polity, 2009.

2005

Rancière, Jacques. *Chronicles of Today's Consensual Times.* Translated by Steve Corcoran. London: Continuum, 2010.

——. *Hatred of Democracy.* Translated by Steve Corcoran. New York: Verso, 2006.

2007

Rancière, Jacques. *The Politics of Literature.* Translated by Julie Rose. Cambridge: Polity, 2011.

2008

Rancière, Jacques. *The Emancipated Spectator.* Translated by Gregory Elliott. London: Verso, 2009.

2009

Rancière, Jacques. *Moments politiques.* Translated by Mary Foster. New York: Seven Stories, 2014.

2010

Rancière, Jacques. *Dissensus: On Politics and Aesthetics.* Translated by Steve Corcoran. London: Continuum, 2010.

2011

Rancière, Jacques. *Aisthesis: Scenes from the Aesthetic Regime of Art.* Translated by Zakir Paul. London: Verso, 2013.

——. *Bela Tarr, the Time After.* Translated by Erik Beranek. Minneapolis: Univocal, 2013.

——. *The Intervals of Cinema.* Translated by John Howe. London: Verso, 2014.

2012

Rancière, Jacques. *Figures of History.* Translated by Julie Rose. Cambridge: Polity, 2014.

——. *The Method of Equality: Interview with Laurent Jeanpierre and Dork Zabunyan.* Cambridge: Polity, 2015.

2014

Rancière, Jacques. *Le fil perdu.* Paris: La Fabrique, 2014.

## Journal Articles and Book Chapters

Rancière, Jacques. "The Aesthetic Dimension: Aesthetics, Politics, Knowledge." *Critical Inquiry* 36, no. 1 (2009): 1–19.

——. "The Aesthetic Heterotopia." *Philosophy Today* 54 (2010): 15–25.

——. "The Aesthetic Revolution and Its Outcomes: Emplotments of Autonomy and Heteronomy." *New Left Review* 14 (2002): 133–151.

——. "Aesthetics Against Incarnation: An Interview by Anne Marie Oliver." *Critical Inquiry* 35 (2008): 172–190.

——. "Aesthetics and Politics Revisited: An Interview with Jacques Rancière." *Critical Inquiry* 38, no. 2 (2012): 289–297.

——. "Aesthetic Separation, Aesthetic Community." *Art and Research: A Journal of Ideas, Contexts and Methods* 2, no. 1 (2008).

——. "Aesthetics, Inaesthetics, Anti-Aesthetics." In *Think Again: Alain Badiou and the Future of Philosophy*, edited by Peter Hallward, 218–231. London: Continuum, 2004.

——. "Art Is Going Elsewhere and Politics Has to Catch It: An Interview with Jacques Rancière." *Krisis* 9, no. 1 (2008): 70–76.

——. "Art of the Possible: Fulvia Carnevale and John Kelsey in Conversation with Jacques Rancière." *Artforum* 45, no. 7 (2007): 256–269.

——. "The Cause of the Other." Translated by David Macey. *Parallax* 4, no. 2 (1998): 25–33.

——. "Comments and Responses." *Theory and Event* 6, no. 4 (2003).

——. "Communists Without Communism." In *The Idea of Communism*, edited by Costas Douzinas and Slavoj Žižek. London: Verso, 2010.

——. "Contemporary Art and the Politics of Aesthetics." In *Communities of Sense: Rethinking Aesthetics and Politics*, edited by Beth Hinderliter et al., 31–50. Durham: Duke University Press, 2009.

——. "Democracies Against Democracy." In *Democracy in What State?*, by Giorgio Agamben et al., translated by William McCuaig, 76–81. New York: Columbia University Press, 2011.

——. "Democracy, Anarchism and Radical Politics Today: An Interview with Jacques Rancière." *Anarchist Studies* 16, no. 2 (2008): 173–185.

——. "Democracy, Dissensus and the Aesthetics of Class Struggle." *Historical Materialism* 13, no. 4 (2005): 285–301.

——. "Discovering New Worlds: Politics of Travel and Metaphor of Space." In *Travellers' Tales: Narratives of Home and Displacement*, edited by George Robertson et al., 29–37. New York: Routledge, 1994.

——. "Dissenting Words: A Conversation with Jacques Rancière." Translated by Davide Panagia. *Diacritics* 30, no. 2 (2000): 113–126.

——. "Does Democracy Mean Something?" In *Adieu Derrida*, edited by Costas Douzinas, 84–100. New York: Palgrave Macmillan, 2007.

——. "Do Pictures Really Want to Live?" *Culture, Theory, and Critique* 50, nos. 2–3 (2009): 123–132.

——. "The Emancipated Spectator." *Artforum* 45, no. 7 (2007): 271–281.

——. "The Ethical Turn of Aesthetics and Politics." Translated by Jean-Philippe Deranty. *Critical Horizons* 7, no. 1 (2006): 1–20.

——. "From Politics to Aesthetics." *Paragraph* 28, no. 1 (2005): 13–25.

——. "Going to the Expo: The Worker, His Wife and Machines." In *Voices of the People: The Politics and Life of "La Sociale" at the End of the Second Empire*, edited by Adrian Rifkin, 23–44. London: Routledge, 1988.

——. "Good Times, Or, Pleasure at the Barriers." In *Voices of the People: The Politics and Life of "La Sociale" at the End of the Second Empire*, translated by John Moore, edited by Adrian Rifkin, 45–95. London: Routledge, 1988.

——. "How to Use 'Lire le Capital.'" *Economy and Society* 5, no. 3 (1976): 377–384.

——. "How to Use *Lire le Capital*." Translated by Talal Asad. In *Ideology, Method and Marx*, edited by Ali Rattansi, 181–189. London: Routledge, 1989.

——. "Is There a Deleuzian Aesthetics?" Translated by Radmila Djordjevic. *Qui parle?* 14, no. 2 (2004): 1–14.
——. "Jacques Ranciere and Interdisciplinarity." Interview with Marie-Aude Baronian and Mireille Rosello. Translated by Gregory Elliott. *Art and Research* 2, no. 1, 2008.
——. "Literary Misunderstanding." *Paragraph* 28, no. 2 (2005): 91–103.
——. "Literature, Politics, Aesthetics: Approaches to Democratic Disagreement." Edited by Solange Guénoun, James H. Kavanagh, and Roxanne Lapidus. *SubStance* 29, no. 2 (2000): 3–24.
——. "The Misadventures of Critical Thinking." *Aporia* 24, no. 2 (2007): 22–32.
——. "The Myth of the Artisan: Critical Reflections on a Category of Social History." Translated by David H. Lake. *International Labour and Working Class History* 24 (1983): 1–16. Reprinted in *Work in France: Representations, Meaning, Organization, and Practice*, edited by Steven Laurence Kaplan and Cynthia J. Koepp, 317–334. Ithaca: Cornell University Press, 1986.
——. "Notes on the Photographic Image." *Radical Philosophy: A Journal of Socialist and Feminist Philosophy* 156 (2009): 8–15.
——. "On Medium Specificity and Discipline Crossovers in Modern Art." Interview by Andrew McNamara and Toni Ross. *Australian and New Zealand Journal of Art* 8, no. 1 (2007): 99–107.
——. "On the Theory of Ideology (the Politics of Althusser)." Translated by M. Jordin. *Radical Philosophy* 7, no. 2 (1974): 2–15.
——. "The Order of the City." *Critical Inquiry* 30, no. 2 (2005): 267–291.
——. "Politics, Identification, and Subjectivization." In *The Identity in Question*, edited by John Rajchman. New York: Routledge, 1995.
——. "The Politics of Literature." *SubStance* 33, no. 1 (2004): 10–24.
——. "The Politics of the Spider." *Studies in Romanticism* 50, no. 2 (2011): 239–250.
——. "Problems and Transformation in Critical Art." Translated by Claire Bishop. In *Participation, Documents of Contemporary Art*, edited by Claire Bishop, 83–93. Cambridge, Mass.: MIT Press, 2006.
——. "Reply to Levy." *Telos* 33 (1977).
——. "Should Democracy Come? Ethics and Politics in Derrida." In *Derrida and the Time of the Political*, edited by Pheng Cheah and Suzanne Guerlac, 274–288. Durham: Duke University Press, 2009.
——. "The Space of Words: From Mallarmé to Broodthaers." Translated by M. Phillips. In *Porous Boundaries: Texts and Images in Twentieth-Century French Culture*, edited by Jérôme Game, 41–61. New York: Peter Lang, 2007.

——. "The Sublime from Lyotard to Schiller: Two Readings of Kant and Their Political Significance." *Radical Philosophy* 126 (2004): 8–15.

——. "Ten Theses on Politics." Translated by Davide Panagia and Rachel Bowlby. *Theory and Event* 5, no. 3 (2001).

——. "Theatre of Images." In *La Politique des Images*, edited by Alfredo Jaar, 71–80. Zurich: JRP/Ringier, 2007.

——. "Thinking Between Disciplines: An Aesthetics of Knowledge." Translated by Jon Roffe. *Parrhesia* 1 (2006): 1–12.

——. "The Thinking of Dissensus: Politics and Aesthetics." In *Reading Rancière*, edited by Paul Bowman and Richard Stamp, 1–17. London: Continuum, 2011.

——. "What Does It Mean to Be Un?" *Continuum* 21, no. 4 (2007): 559–569.

——. "Who Is the Subject of the Rights of Man?" *South Atlantic Quarterly* 103, nos. 2–3 (2004): 297–310.

——. "Why Emma Bovary Had to Be Killed." *Critical Inquiry* 34 (2008): 233–248.

——. "You Can't Anticipate Explosions: Jacques Rancière in Conversation with Chto Delat." *Rethinking Marxism: A Journal of Economics, Culture and Society* 20, no. 3 (2008): 402–412.

Rancière, Jacques, and P. Hallward. "Politics and Aesthetics: an Interview." *Angelaki* 8, no. 2 (2003): 191–211.

## STUDIES ON JACQUES RANCIÈRE

### Books

Biesta, Gert, and Charles Bingham. *Jacques Rancière: Education, Truth, Emancipation*. London: Continuum, 2010.

Bowman, Paul. *Rancière and Film*. Edinburgh: Edinburgh University Press, 2013.

Bowman, Paul, and Richard Stamp. *Reading Rancière: Critical Dissensus*. London: Continuum, 2011.

Chambers, Samuel A. *The Lessons of Rancière*. New York: Oxford University Press, 2013.

Cornu, Laurence, and Patrice Vermeren, eds. *La Philosophie Déplacée: Autour de Jacques Rancière: Colloque de Cerisy*. Bourg en Bresse: Horlieu, 2006.

Davis, Oliver. *Jacques Rancière*. Cambridge: Polity, 2011.

——. *Rancière Now: Current Perspectives on Jacques Rancière*. Cambridge: Polity, 2013.

Deranty, Jean-Philippe. *Jacques Rancière: Key Concepts*. Durham: Acumen, 2010.

Deranty, Jean-Philippe, and Alison Ross, eds. *Jacques Rancière and the Contemporary Scene: The Philosophy of Radical Equality*. London: Continuum, 2012.

Hewlett, Nick. *Badiou, Balibar, Rancière: Re-Thinking Emancipation*. London: Continuum, 2007.

Lewis, Tyson Edward. *The Aesthetics of Education: Theatre, Curiosity, and Politics in the Work of Jacques Rancière and Paulo Freire*. London: Bloomsbury Academic, 2014.

May, Todd. *Contemporary Political Movements and the Thought of Jacques Rancière: Equality in Action*. Edinburgh: Edinburgh University Press, 2010.

——. *The Political Thought of Jacques Rancière: Creating Equality*. Philadelphia: University of Pennsylvania Press, 2008.

Plot, Martin. *The Aesthetico-Political: The Question of Democracy in Merleau-Ponty, Arendt, and Rancière*. London: Bloomsbury Academic, 2014.

Rockhill, Gabriel, and Philip Watts, eds. *Jacques Rancière: History, Politics, Aesthetics*. Durham: Duke University Press, 2009.

Simons, Maarten, and Jan Masschelein, eds. *Rancière, Public Education and the Taming of Democracy*. Malden, Mass.: Wiley-Blackwell, 2011.

Tanke, Joseph. *Jacques Rancière: An Introduction*. London: Continuum, 2011.

## Journal Articles

Badiou, Alain. "The Lessons of Jacques Rancière: Knowledge and Power After the Storm." In *Jacques Rancière: History, Politics, Aesthetics*, edited by Gabriel Rockhill and Philip Watts, 30–54. Durham: Duke University Press, 2009.

——. "Rancière and Apolitics." In *Metapolitics*, translated by J. Barker, 114–123. London: Verso, 2005.

——. "Rancière and the Community of Equals." In *Metapolitics*, translated by J. Barker, 107–113. London: Verso, 2005.

Baiocchi, Gianpaolo, and Brian T. Connor. "Politics as Interruption Rancière's Community of Equals and Governmentality." *Thesis Eleven* 117, no. 1 (2013): 89–100.

Barbour, Charles Andrew. "Militants of Truth, Communities of Equality: Badiou and the Ignorant Schoolmaster." *Educational Philosophy and Theory* 42, no. 2 (2010): 251–263.

Bayly, Simon. "Theatre and the Public Badiou, Rancière, Virno." *Radical Philosophy* 157 (2009): 20–29.

Biesta, Gert. "The Ignorant Citizen: Mouffe, Rancière, and the Subject of Democratic Education." *Studies in Philosophy and Education* 30, no. 2 (2011): 141–153.

——. "A New Logic of Emancipation: The Methodology of Jacques Rancière." *Educational Theory* 60, no. 1 (2010): 39–59.

——. "Towards a New 'Logic' of Emancipation: Foucault and Rancière." In *Philosophy of Education*, edited by R. Glass et al., 169–177. Urbana-Champaign, Ill.: Philosophy of Education Society, 2009.

Bingham, Charles. "Settling No Conflict in the Public Place: Truth in Education, and in Rancièrean Scholarship." *Educational Philosophy and Theory* 42, no. 5 (2010): 649–665.

——. "Under the Name of Method: On Jacques Rancière's Presumptive Tautology." *Journal of Philosophy of Education* 43, no. 3 (2009): 405–420.

Boever, Arne De. "Scenes of Aesthetic Education: Rancière, Oedipus, and Notre Musique." *Journal of Aesthetic Education* 46, no. 3 (2012): 69–82.

Brown, Nathan. "Red Years: Althusser's Lesson, Rancière's Error and the Real Movement of History." *Radical Philosophy* 170 (2011): 16.

Chambers, Samuel A. "Jacques Rancière and the Problem of Pure Politics." *European Journal of Political Theory* 10, no. 3 (2011): 303–326.

——. "Jacques Rancière's Lesson on the Lesson." *Educational Philosophy and Theory* 45, no. 6 (2012): 637–646.

Craib, Ian. "Rancière and Althusser." *Radical Philosophy* 10 (1975): 28–29.

Dasgupta, Sudeep. "Conjunctive Times, Disjointed Time: Philosophy Between Enigma and Disagreement." *Parallax* 15, no. 3 (2009): 3–19.

——. "Jacques Rancière." In *Film, Theory and Philosophy: The Key Thinkers*, edited by F. Colman, chap. 31. Durham: Acumen, 2009.

Davis, Oliver. "Rancière and Queer Theory: On Irritable Attachment." *Borderlands* 8, no. 2 (2009).

Déotte, Jean-Louis, and Roxanne Lapidus. "The Differences Between Rancière's 'Mésentente' (Political Disagreement) and Lyotard's 'Différend.'" *SubStance* 33, no. 1 (2004): 77–90.

Deranty, Jean-Philippe. "Democratic Aesthetics: On Jacques Rancière's Latest Work." *Critical Horizons* 8, no. 2 (2007): 230–255.

——. "Jacques Rancière's Contribution to the Ethics of Recognition." *Political Theory* 31, no. 1 (2003): 136–156.

——. "Rancière and Contemporary Political Ontology." *Theory and Event* 6, no. 4 (2003).

Dillon, Michael. "(De)void of Politics: A Response to Jacques Rancière's Ten Theses on Politics." *Theory and Event* 6, no. 4 (2003).

——. "A Passion for the (Im)possible: Jacques Rancière, Equality, Pedagogy and the Messianic." *European Journal of Political Theory* 4 (2005): 429–452.

Faulkner, Joanne. "Negotiating Vulnerability Through 'Animal' and 'Child' Agamben and Rancière at the Limit of Being Human." *Angelaki* 16, no. 4 (2011): 73–85.

Ferris, David. "Politics After Aesthetics: Disagreeing with Rancière." *Parallax* 15, no. 3 (2009): 37–49.

Galloway, Sarah. "Reconsidering Emancipatory Education: Staging a Conversation Between Paulo Freire and Jacques Rancière." *Educational Theory* 62, no. 2 (2012): 163–184.

Garneau, Michèle, and James Cisneros. "Film's Aesthetic Turn: A Contribution from Jacques Rancière." *SubStance* 33, no. 1 (2004): 108–125.

Gibson, Andrew. "The Unfinished Song: Intermittency and Melancholy in Rancière." *Paragraph* 28, no. 1 (2005): 61–76.

Guénoun, Solange. "An Interview with Jacques Rancière: Cinematographic Image, Democracy, and the 'Splendor of the Insignificant.'" *Journal of Twentieth-Century Contemporary French Studies* 4, no. 2 (2000): 249–258.

——. "Jacques Ranciere's Freudian Cause." *SubStance* 33, no. 1 (2004): 25–53.

Gündoğdu, Ayten. "'Perplexities of the Rights of Man': Arendt on the Aporias of Human Rights." *European Journal of Political Theory* 11, no. 1 (2012): 4–24.

Hallward, Peter. "Jacques Rancière and the Subversion of Mastery." *Paragraph* 28, no. 1 (2005): 26–45.

——. "Staging Equality: On Rancière's Theatrocracy." *New Left Review* 37 (2006): 109–129.

Halpern, Richard. "Theater and Democratic Thought: Arendt to Rancière." *Critical Inquiry* 37, no. 3 (2011): 545–572.

Hemel, Ernst van den. "Included But Not Belonging: Badiou and Rancière on Human Rights." *Krisis* 3 (2008): 16–30.

Hirst, Paul. "Rancière, Ideology and Capital." In *On Law and Ideology*, 79–95. Basingstoke, UK: Macmillan, 1979.

Howells, Christina. "Rancière, Sartre and Flaubert from the Idiot of the Family to the Politics of Aesthetics." *Symposium* 15, no. 2 (2011): 82–94.

Ieven, Bram. "Heteroreductives—Rancière's Disagreement with Ontology." *Parallax* 15, no. 3 (2009): 50–62.

Ingram, James. "The Subject of the Politics of Recognition: Hannah Arendt and Jacques Rancière." In *Socialité et reconnaissance: Grammaires de l'humain*, edited by G. Bertram et al., 229–245. Paris: L'Harmattan, 2006.

Israel-Pelletier, Aimee. "Godard, Rohmer, and Rancière's Phrase-Image." *SubStance* 34, no. 3 (2005): 33–46.

Kingwell, Mark. "Throwing Dice: Luck of the Draw and the Democratic Ideal." *Phaenex* 7, no. 1 (2012): 66–100.

Labelle, Gilles. "Two Refoundation Projects of Democracy in Contemporary French Philosophy: Cornelius Castoriadis and Jacques Rancière." *Philosophy and Social Criticism* 27, no. 4 (2001): 75–103.

Lewis, Tyson Edward. "Education in the Realm of the Senses: Understanding Paulo Freire's Aesthetic Unconscious Through Jacques Rancière." *Journal of Philosophy of Education* 43, no. 2 (2009): 285–329.

——. "Jacques Rancière's Aesthetic Regime and Democratic Education." *Journal of Aesthetic Education* 47, no. 2 (2013): 49–70.

——. "Paulo Freire's Last Laugh: Rethinking Critical Pedagogy's Funny Bone Through Jacques Rancière." *Educational Philosophy and Theory* 42, no. 5 (2010): 635–648.

Love, Jeff, and Todd May. "From Universality to Inequality." *Symposium* 12, no. 2 (2008): 51–69.

Magagnoli, Paolo. "Moulène, Rancière and 24 Objets de Grève: Productive Ambivalence or Reifying Opacity?" *Philosophy of Photography* 3, no. 1 (2012): 155–171.

Masschelein, Jan, and Maarten Simons. "The Hatred of Public Schooling: The School as the Mark of Democracy." *Educational Philosophy and Theory* 42, nos. 5–6 (2010): 666–682.

May, Todd. "Jacques Rancière and the Ethics of Equality." *SubStance* 36, no. 2 (2007): 20–36.

——. "Jacques Rancière: Literature and Equality." *Philosophy Compass* 3, no. 1 (2007): 83–92.

McClure, Kirstie M. "Disconnections, Connections and Questions: Reflections on Jacques Rancière's Ten Theses on Politics." *Theory and Event* 6, no. 4 (2003).

McQuillan, Colin. "The Intelligence of Sense: Rancière's Aesthetics." *Symposium* 15, no. 2 (2011): 11–27.

Méchoulan, Eric. "Introduction: On the Edges of Jacques Rancière." *SubStance* 33, no. 1 (2004): 3–9.

Mercieca, Duncan. "Initiating 'The Methodology of Jacques Rancière': How Does It All Start?" *Studies in Philosophy and Education* 31, no. 4 (2012): 407–417.

Mufti, Aamir. "Reading Jacques Rancière's Ten Theses on Politics: After September 11th." *Theory and Event* 6, no. 4 (2003).

Munster, Rens van. "Rancière." In *Critical Theorists and International Relations*, edited by Jenny Edkins and Nick Vaughan-Williams, 266–277. London: Routledge, 2009.

Newmark, Kevin. "A Poetics of Sharing: Political Economy in a Prose Poem by Baudelaire." *Symposium* 15, no. 2 (2011): 57–81.

Panagia, Davide. "Ceci n'est pas un argument: An Introduction to the Ten Theses." *Theory and Event* 5, no. 3 (2001).

——. "Thinking With and Against 'Ten Theses.'" *Theory and Event* 6, no. 4 (2003).

Pelletier, Caroline. "Emancipation, Equality and Education: Rancière's Critique of Bourdieu and the Question of Performativity." *Discourse: Studies in the Cultural Politics of Education* 30, no. 2 (2009): 137–150.

——. "Rancière and the Poetics of the Social Sciences." *International Journal of Research and Method in Education* 32, no. 3 (2009): 267–284.

Phillips, Chas. "Difference, Disagreement and the Thinking of Queerness." *Borderlands* 8, no. 2 (2009).

Phillips, John W. P. "Art, Politics and Philosophy: Alain Badiou and Jacques Rancière." *Theory, Culture and Society* 27, no. 4 (2010): 146–160.

Power, Nina. "Non-Reproductive Futurism: Rancière's Rational Equality Against Edelman's Body Apolitic." *Borderlands* 8, no. 2 (2009).

——. "Which Equality? Badiou and Rancière in Light of Feuerbach." *Parallax* 15, no. 3 (2009): 63–80.

Renault, Emmanuel. "The Many Marx of Jacques Rancière." In *Jacques Rancière and the Contemporary Scene: The Philosophy of Radical Equality*, edited by Jean-Philippe Deranty and Alison Ross, 167–186. New York: Continuum, 2012.

Rifkin, Adrian. "Il y a des mots qu'on ne souhaiterait plus lire." *Paragraph* 28, no. 1 (2005): 96–109.

——. "JR Cinéphile, or the Philosopher Who Loved Things." *Parallax* 15, no. 3 (2009): 81–87.

——. "Oh I Do Like to Be Beside the Seaside (Now Voyager) . . . : On Misunderstanding Rancière and Queer Theory." *Borderlands* 8, no. 2 (2009).

Robson, Mark. "Jacques Rancière's Aesthetic Communities." *Paragraph* 28, no. 1 (2005): 77–95.

——. "'A Literary Animal': Rancière, Derrida, and the Literature of Democracy." *Parallax* 15, no. 3 (2009): 88–101.

Rockhill, Gabriel. "Rancière's Productive Contradictions: From the Politics of Aesthetics to the Social Politicity of the Artistic Practice." *Symposium* 15, no. 2 (2011): 28–56.

Ross, Alison. "The Aesthetic Fable: Cinema in Jacques Rancière's 'Aesthetic Politics.'" *SubStance* 38, no. 1 (2009): 128–150.

Ross, Kristin. "Rancière and the Practice of Equality." *Social Text* 29 (1991): 57–71.

Ruitenberg, Claudia. "Queer Politics in Schools: A Rancièrean Reading." *Educational Philosophy and Theory* 42, no. 5 (2010): 618–634.

Schaap, Andrew. "Enacting the Right to Have Rights: Jacques Rancière's Critique of Hannah Arendt." *European Journal of Political Theory* 10, no. 1 (2011): 22–45.

Shapiro, Michael. "Radicalising Democratic Theory: Social Space in Connolly, Deleuze and Rancière." In *The New Pluralism: William Connolly and the Contemporary Global Condition*, edited by David Campbell and Morton Schoolman, 197–220. Durham: Duke University Press, 2008.

Shaw, Devin Zane. "Cartesian Egalitarianism: From Poullain de la Barre to Rancière." *Phaenex* 7, no. 1 (2012): 101–129.

——. "The Nothingness of Equality: The 'Sartrean Existentialism' of Jacques Rancière." *Sartre Studies International* 18, no. 1 (2012): 29–48.

Sonderegger, Ruth. "Negative Versus Affirmative Critique: On Pierre Bourdieu and Jacques Rancière." In *Conceptions of Critique in Modern and Contemporary Philosophy*, edited by Ruth Sonderegger and Karin de Boer, 248–264. London: Palgrave Macmillan, 2012.

Stamp, Richard. "Of Slumdogs and Schoolmasters: Jacotot, Rancière and Mitra on Self-Organized Learning." *Educational Philosophy and Theory* 45, no. 6 (2012): 647–662.

——. "The Torsion of Politics and Friendship in Derrida, Foucault and Rancière." *Borderlands* 8, no. 2 (2009).

Stoneman, Ethan. "Appropriate Indecorum Rhetoric and Aesthetics in the Political Theory of Jacques Rancière." *Philosophy and Rhetoric* 44, no. 2 (2011): 129–149.

Tambakaki, Paulina. "When Does Politics Happen?" *Parallax* 15, no. 3 (2009): 102–113.

Tanke, Joseph. "Why Rancière Now?" *Journal of Aesthetic Education* 44, no. 2 (2009): 1–17.

Trott, Adriel. "Rancière and Aristotle: Parapolitics, Part-y Politics and the Institution of Perpetual Politics." *Journal for Speculative Philosophy* 26, no. 4 (2012): 627–646.

Ulary, Georganna. "Rancière, Kristeva and the Rehabilitation of Political Life." *Thesis Eleven* 106, no. 1 (2011): 23–38.

Valentine, Jeremy. "Rancière and Contemporary Political Problems." *Paragraph* 28, no. 1 (2005): 46–60.

White, Hayden. "Foreword: Rancière's Revisionism." In *The Names of History: On the Poetics of Knowledge*, by Jacques Rancière, translated by H. Hassan Melehy, vii–xx. Minneapolis: University of Minnesota Press, 1994.

Wolfe, Katharine. "From Aesthetics to Politics: Rancière, Kant and Deleuze." *Contemporary Aesthetics* 4 (2006).

Žižek, Slavoj. "Political Subjectivization and Its Vicissitudes." In *The Ticklish Subject*, 171–244. London: Verso, 1999.

## Other Works Cited

Adorno, Theodor W. *Negative Dialectics*. Translated by E. B. Ashton. London: Routledge, 1973.

Adorno, Theodor W., and Max Horkheimer, *Dialectic of Enlightenment*. Translated by Edmund Jephcott. Stanford: Stanford University Press, 2002.

Allen, Amy. *The Politics of Ourselves*. New York: Columbia University Press, 2008.

Althusser, Louis, "Ideology and State Apparatuses: Notes Towards an Investigation." In *Lenin and Philosophy, and Other Essays*, translated by Ben Brewster. New York: Monthly Review Press, 1971.

Althusser, Louis, Roger Establet, Pierre Macherey, and Étienne Balibar. *Reading Capital*. Translated by Ben Brewster. New York: Verso, 2009.

Arendt, Hannah. *The Human Condition*. Chicago: University of Chicago Press, 1958.

——. *The Origins of Totalitarianism*. New York: Meridian, 1961.

Avenshen, Samantha, and David Owen. *Foucault Contra Habermas: Recasting the Dialogue Between Genealogy and Critical Theory*. London: Sage, 1999.

Badiou, Alain. *Being and Event*. Translated by Oliver Feltham. New York: Continuum, 2005.

——. *L'hypothèse communiste*. Paris: Lignes, 2009.

——. *Metapolitics*. Translated by Jason Barker. New York: Verso, 2005.

——. *Theory of the Subject*. Translated by Bruno Bosteels. London: Continuum, 2009.

Balibar, Étienne. *Equaliberty*. Translated by James Ingram. Durham: Duke University Press, 2014.

——. *Masses, Classes, Ideas: Studies on Politics and Philosophy Before and After Marx*. Translated by James Swenson. New York: Routledge, 1994.

Berlin, Isaiah. *Four Essays on Liberty*. Oxford: Oxford University Press, 1990.

Blickle, Peter. *Die Revolution von 1525*. Oldenburg: Oldenburg Wissenschaftsverlag, 2004.

Boltanski, Luc. *On Critique: A Sociology of Emancipation.* Translated by Gregory Elliott. Cambridge: Polity, 2011.

Boltanski, Luc, and Eve Chiapello. *The New Spirit of Capitalism.* Translated by Gregory Elliott. London: Verso, 2007.

Borradori, Giovanna. *Philosophy in a Time of Terror: Dialogues with Jürgen Habermas and Jacques Derrida.* Chicago: University of Chicago Press, 2003.

Boucher, Geoff. "The Politics of Aesthetic Affect: A Reconstruction of Habermas's Art Theory." *Parrhesia* 13 (2011): 62–78.

Bourdieu, Pierre. *Weight of the World: Social Suffering in Contemporary Society.* Cambridge: Polity, 1999.

Brauer, Susanne. *Natur und Sittlichkeit: Die Familie in Hegels Rechtsphilosophie.* Freiburg: Karl Alber Verlag, 2007.

Brunkhorst, Hauke. *Solidarity: From Civic Friendship to a Global Legal Community.* Cambridge, Mass.: MIT Press, 2005.

Butler, Judith. *The Psychic Life of Power: Subjection in Theories.* Stanford: Stanford University Press, 1997.

——. "*What Is Critique?* An Essay on Foucault's Virtue." In *The Political*, edited by David Ingram, 212–226. Oxford: Blackwell, 2002.

Butler, Judith, Ernesto Laclau, and Slavoj Žižek. *Contingency, Hegemony, Universality: Contemporary Dialogues on the Left.* London: Verso, 2000.

Butler, Judith, and Catherine Malabou. *Sois mon corps: Une lecture contemporaine de la domination et de la servitude chez Hegel.* Paris: Bayard, 2010.

Colclasure, David. *Habermas and Literary Rationality.* London: Routledge, 2010.

Couzens Hoy, David, and Thomas MacCarthy. *Critical Theory.* Oxford: Wiley-Blackwell, 1994.

Dejours, Christophe. *Souffrance en France: La Banalisation de l'Injustice Sociale.* Paris: Seuil, 1998.

Deleuze, Gilles, and Felix Guattari. *Kafka: Towards a Minor Literature.* Translated by Dana Polan. Minneapolis: University of Minnesota Press, 1986.

——. *A Thousand Plateaus: Capitalism and Schizophrenia.* Translated by Brian Massumi. Minneapolis: University of Minnesota Press, 1987.

Derrida, Jacques. *Of Grammatology.* Translated by Gayatri Chakravorty Spivak. Baltimore: Johns Hopkins University Press, 1978.

——. *Writing and Difference.* Translated by Alan Bass. Chicago: University of Chicago Press, 1978.

Durkheim, Émile. *Professional Ethics and Civic Morals.* Translated by Cornelia Brookfield. London: Routledge, 1992.

Duvenage, Pieter. *Habermas and Aesthetics: The Limits of Communicative Reason.* Cambridge: Polity, 2003.

Emundts, Dina, and Rolf-Peter Horstmann. *G. W. F. Hegel: Eine Einführung.* Stuttgart: Philipp Reclam, 2002.

Engels, Friedrich. *Der Deutsche Bauernkrieg.* In *Karl Marx—Friedrich Engels—Werke*, vol. 7. Berlin: Dietz Verlag, 1960.

Forst, Rainer. *The Right to Justification.* Translated by Jeffrey Flynn. New York: Columbia University Press, 2014.

Foucault, Michel. "*Omnes et Singulatim*: Towards a Critique of Political Reason." In *Tanner Lectures on Human Values*, edited by Sterling M. McMurrin, vol. 2. Cambridge: Cambridge University Press, 1981.

——. "The Subject and Power." in *Michel Foucault: Beyond Structuralism and Hermeneutics*, edited by Hubert Dreyfus and Paul Rabinow, 208–226. Chicago: University of Chicago Press, 1982.

——. "What Is Critique?" In *The Politics of Truth*, edited by Sylvere Lotringer, 41–81. Los Angeles: Semiotext(e), 2007.

——. "What Is Enlightenment?" In *The Foucault Reader*, edited by Paul Rabinow, 32–50. New York: Pantheon, 1984.

Fraser, Nancy. *Justice Interruptus.* New York: Routledge, 1997.

——. "Recognition Without Ethics." *Theory, Culture and Society* 18, nos. 2–3 (2001): 21–42.

——. "Rethinking Recognition." *New Left Review* 3 (2000): 107–120.

——. *Scales of Justice.* New York: Columbia University Press, 2010.

Geuss, Raymond. "Auffassungen der Freiheit." *Zeitschrift für philosophische Forschung* 49 (1995): 1–14.

Gutmann, Amy. *Liberal Equality.* Cambridge: Cambridge University Press, 1980.

Habermas, Jürgen. *Between Facts and Norms.* Translated by William Rehg. Cambridge: Polity, 1996.

——. *Knowledge and Human Interests.* Translated by Jeremy J. Shapiro. Cambridge: Polity, 1987.

Hegel, Georg Wilhelm Friedrich. *Aesthetics: Lectures on Fine Art.* Oxford: Clarendon, 1988.

——. *Elements of the Philosophy of Right.* Translated by H. B. Nisbet. Cambridge: Cambridge University Press, 2008.

——. *Lectures on the Philosophy of World History.* Translated by H. B. Nisbet. Cambridge: Cambridge University Press, 1984.

——. *Philosophie des Rechts: Die Vorlesung von 1819/20 in einer Nachschrift.* Frankfurt: Suhrkamp, 1983.

——. *Philosophy of Mind.* Translated by Michael Inwood. Oxford: Oxford University Press, 2010.

Hengen Fox, Nicholas. "A Habermasian Literary Criticism." *New Literary History* 43, no. 2 (2012): 235–254.

Henrich, Dieter. *Fixpunkte: Abhandlungen und Essays zur Theorie der Kunst.* Frankfurt: Suhrkamp, 2003.

Hirschman, Albert O. *Exit, Voice, and Loyalty: Responses to Decline in Firms, Organizations, and States.* Cambridge, Mass.: Harvard University Press, 1970.

Honig, Bonnie. *Antigone Interrupted.* Cambridge: Cambridge University Press, 2013.

Honneth, Axel, and Martin Saar. *Michel Foucault: Zwischenbilanz einer Rezeption: Frankfurter Foucault Konferenz 2001.* Frankfurt: Suhrkamp, 2003.

Horkheimer, Max. *Between Philosophy and Social Science.* Translated by F. Hunter, M. Kramer, and J. Torpey. Cambridge, Mass.: MIT Press, 1993.

——. "Traditional and Critical Theory." In *Critical Theory: Selected Essays*, translated by Matthew J. O'Connell and others, 188–243. New York: Continuum, 2002.

Ikäheimo, Heikki. *Anerkennung.* Berlin: De Gruyter, 2014.

——. "Holism and Normative Essentialism in Hegel's Social Ontology." In *Recognition and Social Ontology*, edited by Heikki Ikäheimo and Arto Laitinen, 145–209. Leiden: Brill, 2011.

Kelly, Michael. *Critique and Power: Recasting the Foucault/Habermas Debate.* Studies in Contemporary German Social Thought. Cambridge, Mass.: MIT Press, 1994.

Kompridis, Nikolas. *Critique and Disclosure: Critical Theory Between Past and Future.* Cambridge, Mass.: MIT Press, 2006.

Laitinen, Arto, and Birgitta Pessi, eds. *Solidarity: Theory and Practice.* Lanham, Md.: Lexington Books, 2014.

Lyotard, Jean-François. *The Differend: Phrases in Dispute.* Translated by George Van Den Abeele. Minneapolis: University of Minnesota Press, 1989.

——. *The Postmodern Condition: A Report on Knowledge.* Translated by Geoff Bennington and Brian Massumi. Minneapolis: University of Minnesota Press, 1984.

Marx, Karl. *Capital I.* Translated by Ben Fowkes. London: Penguin, 1990.

McNay, Lois. *The Misguided Search for the Political.* London: Polity, 2014.

Menke, Christoph. "Geist und Leben: Zu einer genealogischen Kritik der Phänomenologie." In *Von der Logik zur Sprache: Stuttgarter Hegel-Kongress 2005*, edited by Rudiger Bubner and G. Hindrichs, 321–348. Stuttgart: Klett-Cotta, 2005.

Neuhouser, Frederick. *Foundations of Hegel's Social Theory: Actualizing Freedom.* Cambridge, Mass.: Harvard University Press, 2000.

Nielsen, Kai. *Equality and Liberty: A Defence of Radical Egalitarianism.* Totowa, N.J.: Rowman and Allanheld, 1985.

Peden, Knox. *Spinoza Contra Phenomenology: French Rationalism from Cavaillès to Deleuze.* Stanford: Stanford University Press, 2014.

Pippin, Robert B. *Hegel's Practical Philosophy: Rational Agency as Ethical Life.* Cambridge: Cambridge University Press, 2008.

Priddat, Birger P. *Hegel als Ökonom.* Berlin: Duncker und Humblot, 1990.

Rajchman, John. *The Identity in Question.* New York: Routledge: 1995.

Renault, Emmanuel. "A Critical Theory of Social Suffering." *Critical Horizons* 11, no. 2 (2010): 221–241.

——. *L'expérience de l'injustice: Reconnaissance et clinique de l'injustice.* Paris: La Découverte, 2004.

——. *Souffrances sociales: Sociologie, psychologie, politique.* Paris: La Découverte, 2008.

Ross, Alison. *Walter Benjamin's Concept of the Image.* New York: Routledge, 2014.

Schiavone, Aldo. *Spartacus.* Cambridge, Mass.: Harvard University Press, 2013.

Sen, Amartya. *Inequality Reexamined.* Cambridge, Mass.: Harvard University Press, 1995.

Siep, Ludwig. *Praktische Philosophie im Deutschen Idealismus.* Frankfurt: Suhrkamp, 1992.

Simons, Jon, ed. *Contemporary Critical Theorists: From Agamben to Žižek.* Edinburgh: Edinburgh University Press, 2010.

——, ed. *Contemporary Critical Theorists: From Lacan to Said.* Edinburgh: Edinburgh University Press, 2004.

Sinnerbrink, Robert, Jean-Philippe Deranty, Nicholas Smith, and Peter Schmiedgen. *Critique Today.* Leiden: Brill, 2006.

Taylor, Charles. "The Politics of Recognition." In *Multiculturalism*, edited by Amy Gutmann. Princeton: Princeton University Press, 1994.

Theunissen, Michael. "The Repressed Intersubjectivity in Hegel's Philosophy of Right." In *Hegel and Legal Theory*, edited by Drucilla Cornell, Michel Rosenfeld, and David Carlson, 3–63. New York: Routledge, 1991.

——. "Society and History: A Critique of Critical Theory." In *Habermas: A Critical Reader*, edited by P. Dews, 241–271. Oxford: Blackwell, 1999.

Thomassen, Lasse. *The Derrida-Habermas Reader.* Chicago: University of Chicago Press, 2006.

Tully, James. *On Global Citizenship: Dialogue with James Tully*. London: Bloomsbury Academic, 2014.

——. *Philosophy in a New Key*. Cambridge: Cambridge University Press, 2008.

Wellmer, Albrecht. *The Persistence of Modernity: Essays on Aesthetics, Ethics and Postmodernism*. Translated by David Midgley. Cambridge, Mass.: MIT Press, 1991.

Whitebook, Joel. "Die Grenzen des *intersubjective turn*: Eine Erwiederung auf Axel Honneth." *Psyché: Zeitschrift für Psychoanalyse und ihre Anwendungen*, edited by Werner Bohleber, 3 (2003).

——. "Mutual Recognition and the Work of the Negative." In *Pluralism and the Pragmatic Turn: The Transformation of Critical Theory: Essays in Honor of Thomas McCarthy*, edited by William Regh and James Bohman, 257–291. Cambridge, Mass.: MIT Press, 2001.

——. *Perversion and Utopia: A Study in Psychoanalysis and Critical Theory*. Cambridge, Mass.: MIT Press, 1995.

Whyte, Jessica. *Catastrophe and Redemption: The Political Thought of Giorgio Agamben*. New York: State University of New York Press, 2014.

Young, Iris Marion. *Justice and the Politics of Difference*. Princeton: Princeton University Press, 1990.

Zerilli, Linda. *Feminism and the Abyss of Freedom*. Chicago: University of Chicago Press, 2005.

# INDEX

## NEW DIRECTIONS IN CRITICAL THEORY

Amy Allen, General Editor

*Mute Speech: Literature, Critical Theory, and Politics*, Jacques Rancière

*The Right to Justification: Elements of Constructivist Theory of Justice*, Rainer Forst

*The Scandal of Reason: A Critical Theory of Political Judgment*, Albena Azmanova

*The Wrath of Capital: Neoliberalism and Climate Change Politics*, Adrian Parr

*Media of Reason: A Theory of Rationality*, Matthias Vogel

*Social Acceleration: The Transformation of Time in Modernity*, Hartmut Rosa

*The Disclosure of Politics: Struggles Over the Semantics of Secularization*, María Pía Lara

*Radical Cosmopolitics: The Ethics and Politics of Democratic Universalism*, James Ingram

*Freedom's Right: The Social Foundations of Democratic Life*, Axel Honneth

*Imaginal Politics: Images Beyond Imagination and the Imaginary*, Chiara Bottici

*Alienation*, Rahel Jaeggi

*The Power of Tolerance: A Debate*, Wendy Brown and Rainer Forst, edited by Luca Di Blasi and Christoph F. E. Holzhey

*Radical History and the Politics of Art*, Gabriel Rockhill

*The Highway of Despair: Critical Theory After Hegel*, Robyn Marasco

*A Political Economy of the Senses: Neoliberalism, Reification, Critique*, Anita Chari

*The End of Progress: Decolonizing the Normative Foundations of Critical Theory*, Amy Allen